T0212565

Communications
in Computer and Information Science   486

More information about this series at http://www.springer.com/series/7899

Martin Ebner · Kai Erenli
Rainer Malaka · Johanna Pirker
Aaron E. Walsh (Eds.)

Immersive Education

4th European Summit, EiED 2014
Vienna, Austria, November 24–26, 2014
Revised Selected Papers

 Springer

Editors
Martin Ebner
Graz University of Technology
Graz
Austria

Kai Erenli
University of Applied Sciences bfi Vienna
Vienna
Austria

Rainer Malaka
University of Bremen
Bremen
Germany

Johanna Pirker
Graz University of Technology
Graz
Austria

Aaron E. Walsh
Boston College
Boston, MA
USA

ISSN 1865-0929   ISSN 1865-0937   (electronic)
Communications in Computer and Information Science
ISBN 978-3-319-22016-1   ISBN 978-3-319-22017-8   (eBook)
DOI 10.1007/978-3-319-22017-8

Library of Congress Control Number: 2015945146

Springer Cham Heidelberg New York Dordrecht London
© Springer International Publishing Switzerland 2015

Printed on acid-free paper

Springer International Publishing AG Switzerland is part of Springer Science+Business Media
(www.springer.com)

Preface

Immersive Education has been an active topic of interest for educators, researchers, and businesses for nearly a decade. As the enabling technologies continue to evolve, immersive scenarios and environments are increasingly becoming more mainstream. What once had to be developed, deployed, and maintained by specialists can now be created by a broad and largely non-technical audience.

Ongoing research scenarios range from architectural applications such as previsualization and augmented enhancements to data goggles and game-based learning. In order to discuss upcoming topics and research results Immersive Education (iED) Summits were established in 2005. As organizer serves the Immersive Education Initiative, a non-profit international collaboration of educational institutions, research institutes, museums, consortia, and companies.

Immersive Education Summits (iED Summits) are official Immersive Education Initiative conferences organized for educators, researchers, administrators, business leaders, and the general public. iED Summits consist of a broad variety of presentations, panel discussions, break-out sessions, demos, and workshops that provide attendees with an in-depth overview of immersion as well as the technologies that enable immersive scenarios, experiences, and environments. iED Summits feature new and emerging virtual worlds, game-based learning and training systems, simulations, virtual reality and mixed/augmented reality, fully immersive environments, immersive learning and training platforms, cutting-edge research from around the world, and related tools, techniques, technologies, standards, and best practices.

Building on the previous 8 years of Immersive Education conferences, the 4th European Immersive Education Summit (EiED 2014) was organized in conjunction with the University of Applied Sciences bfi Vienna, Graz University of Technology (both Austria), and the University of Bremen (Germany). The theme of the 4th European Immersive Education Summit was "Science Meets Business – From Innovative Research to Successful Services and Products."

The summit brought together highly qualified experts from more than 13 countries. The acceptance rate was 62 % in order to aim for a high quality of work. The summit also hosted a location-based learning game that actively engaged participants in an immersive sightseeing and learning experience that took place throughout the Inner City of Vienna.

This book in your hands contains the final best research papers presented at the 4th European Immersive Education Summit. After a double-blind peer review process we carefully selected publications with the best feedback and ranking. Authors of the top-ranked papers were invited to extend their publications and submit them to be included in this book. You will find interesting research studies from a broad research field.

The research study in "A Contribution to Collaborative Learning Using iPads for School Children" aims toward enhancing the learning experience, stimulating communication and cooperative behavior to improve learning. Making use of recent technological advancements (tablets) and gaming as a motivational factor, a prototype application in the form of a multiplayer learning game for iPads was designed and developed. An initial field study at two primary schools in Graz showed promising results for the learning behavior of school children.

The paper "Mining and Visualizing Usage of Educational Systems Using Linked Data" introduces a case study on usage of semantic context modeling and creation of linked data from logs in educational systems like a personal learning environment (PLE) with a focus on improvements and monitoring such systems, in general, with respect to social-, functional-, user-, and activity-centric levels.

The work in "Determining the Causing Factors of Errors for Multiplication Problems" detects the difficulty levels within a set of multiplication problems and analyzes the dataset on different error types as described and determined in several pedagogical surveys and investigations.

The paper "Tutoring Teachers – Building an Online Tutoring Platform for Teachers' Community" elaborates on the design, the first prototype, and an early evaluation of the Go-Lab Tutoring Platform.

In the study presented in "Towards Digital Immersive and Seamless Language Learning," the authors investigate the potential of new technologies and want to find out how immersion teaching is supported through seamless learning approaches.

In "How to Detect Programming Skills of Students" the authors focus on designing the technique to detect and recognize programming patterns from student's program source codes. Finally, they propose some use cases and further directions of their research.

"Binding Daily Physical Environments to Learning Activities with Mobile and Sensor Technology" presents the NFC LearnTracker, a mobile tool proposing that the user introspect his/her autobiography as a learner to identify successful physical learning environments, mark them with sensor tags, bind them to self-defined learning goals, keep track of the time invested on each goal with a natural interface, and monitor the learning analytics.

The paper "Immersive Installation: "A Virtual St. Kilda" discusses a Virtual Histories project, which developed a digital reconstruction of the St. Kilda archipelago. The simulation covers 4 km^2 of virtual space, and models both tangible and intangible culture.

"Mobile Exploration of Medieval St. Andrews" presents work that explores using mobile technologies to support investigation, learning, and appreciation of the past. It builds on tradition and world-class scholarship into the history of this important town and makes them available to school students, researchers, and tourists using mobile technologies.

"Theoretical Issues for Game-Based Virtual Heritage" critiques essential features in prominent theories of serious games, and compares them with interaction features of commercial computer games that could be used for history and heritage-based learning in order to develop heuristics that may help the specific requirements of serious game design for interactive history and digital heritage.

"GAMEDUCATION: Using Gamification Techniques to Engage Learners in Online Learning" reviews theories and research related to learner motivation and engagement. Moreover, it proposes using Gamification in the context of education to tackle the lack of learners' engagement.

We would like to express our gratitude to all supporters of the conference as well as the chairs, reviewers, contributors, and organizers. We are equally indebted to all helping hands before and during the event.

Additionally we would like to thank everyone who made this book such a great resource. Their names are listed herein.

November 2014

Martin Ebner
Kai Erenli
Rainer Malaka
Johanna Pirker
Aaron E. Walsh

Organization

General Chairs

Rainer Malaka	University of Bremen, Germany
Kai Erenli	University of Applied Science bfi Vienna, Austria
Martin Ebner	Graz University of Technology, Austria
Johanna Pirker	Graz University of Technology, Austria
Aaron E. Walsh	Immersive Education Initiative and Boston College, USA

Organizing Committee

Roxane Koitz	Graz University of Technology, Austria
Angelika Sönnichsen	University of Applied Science bfi Vienna, Austria

Program Committee

Dietrich Albert	University of Graz, Austria
Colin Allison	University of St. Andrews, UK
Mohammad Al-Smadi	Tallinn University, Estonia
Leena Arhippainen	Center for Internet Excellence, Finland
Juan Carlos Augusto	Middlesex University, UK
Theo Bastiaens	Open University Hagen, Germany
Marcus Birkenkrahe	HWR Berlin, Germany
Pierre Bourdin	University of Barcelona, Spain
Manuel Castro	Universidad Nacional de Educación a Distancia, Spain
J. Cecil	Oklahoma State University, USA
Erik Champion	Curtin University, Australia
Vanessa Chang	Curtin University, Australia
Jennifer DeBoer	Massachusetts Institute of Technology, USA
Sara de Freitas	Curtin University, Australia
Nellie Deutsch	Ort Hermelin College of Engineering, Israel
Jon Dron	Athabasca University, Canada
Henry Been-Lirn Duh	University of Tasmania, Australia
Eric Duval	KU Leuven, Belgium
Martin Ebner	Graz University of Technology, Austria
Justin Ehrlich	Western Illinois University, USA
Jennifer Elliott	University of Cincinnati, USA
Kai Erenli	University of Applied Science bfi Vienna, Austria
Baltasar Fernandez-Manjon	Universidad Carlos III de Madrid, Spain
Bekim Fetaji	South East European University, Macedonia

Contents

Innovation and Technological Advancements in E-Learning

A Contribution to Collaborative Learning Using IPads for School Children

Martin Ebner(✉) and Benedikt Kienleitner

Social Learning, Graz University of Technology, Graz, Austria
martin.ebner@tugraz.at, b.kienleitner@gmail.com

Abstract. Collaboration has a very positive effect on students' learning experiences as well as their social interactions. Our research study aims towards enhancing the learning experience, stimulating communication and cooperative behavior to improve learning. Making use of recent technological advancements (tablets) and gaming as a motivational factor, a prototype application in form of a multiplayer learning game for iPads was designed and developed. In a face-to-face setting, connecting up to four devices, the players (learners) have to solve word puzzles in a collaborative way. Furthermore, a web-interface for teachers provides the possibility to create custom content as well as to receive feedback of the children's performance. A first field study at two primary schools in Graz showed promising results for the learning behavior of school children.

Keywords: Cooperation · Learning · School · Communication · Gamification

1 Introduction

The last decade has provided us with amazing new and innovative technological possibilities. New ways to deliver content and support learning have become available whether on the software side, named Web 2.0 [1], as well on the hardware side like the development of smartphones and tablets. In addition, computers, and tablets in particular, offer a perfect opportunity to present learning material in a more playful manner. Under the right circumstances, especially education with learning games can have many benefits [2].

While there are a lot of educational games for mobile devices out there, we could only find a handful that focus on the aspect of communication and cooperation among peers. As it has been shown in numerous studies [3], collaborative learning can have a positive effect on social behavior as well as learning results and communication abilities [4, 5]. Due to the fact that learning is an active on part of the learner where knowledge and understanding is constructed by the learner [6], communication and collaboration are essential factors for this process. Learning is a highly social process and develops through conversation [7, 8].

2 Research Goal

Focusing on the aspect of cooperation and collaborative learning, our research goal is to use digital devices to connect the learners to strongly assist the communication between peers. The fundamental idea is to develop an application where learners actively engage into collaborative work.

M. Ebner et al. (Eds): EiED 2014, CCIS 486, pp. 3–16, 2015.
DOI: 10.1007/978-3-319-22017-8_1

During the course of the following pages, we will present some theoretical background and experiences on cooperative learning with mobile devices, the design of our application and finally the results of the first field tests in two elementary school classes.

3 Theoretical Background

As a first step we want to share some information on collaborative learning, educational games and the use of mobile devices in classrooms.

3.1 Collaborative Learning

In simple terms, collaborative learning can be described as a situation in which two or more people attempt to learn something together [9]. They will ask each other for information, evaluate one another's ideas and monitor one another's work [10]. The benefits are an increase in students' engagement and their motivation to learn as well as a deeper understanding of learning material [11, 12]. Furthermore, as a result of collaboration and communication among peers, an improvement of students' interpersonal relationships was noticed [3].

3.2 Educational Games

Outside school, computer games have become an integral part of young people's live, holding a special fascination and provoking a deep sense of engagement [13]. The motivational aspect of gaming can be combined with curricular contents, creating games with educational purpose. Learning in that matter is believed to be more learner-centered, easier, more enjoyable, interesting and thus more effective [14, 15].

Today there are numerous research studies carrying out the idea of using games for learning [16–19] and pointing out how learning can be improved through using the three crucial factors: curiosity, fantasy and challenge [13].

3.3 Mobile Devices in Classrooms

There are two key factors for the use of mobile devices in classrooms [20]:

- One device per student.
- A communication network that supports peer-to-peer connections and/or internet connectivity.

In such an environment, handheld devices can have numerous educational benefits, a few of them are listed below [21]:

- Portability. The ease of movement with the device creates learning environments that have not been possible before.

- Social interactivity through wireless communication. Peer-to-peer communication makes data exchange, face-to-face interaction and collaboration possible.
- Connectivity, establishing a shared environment for data collection among distributed devices.

In recent years there has been a trend towards an integral use of handheld devices in classrooms instead of the occasional visit of computer labs. Portability and peer-to-peer connectivity make them a perfect choice to assist cooperative learning approaches. Thus, the collaboration of students through different mobile devices has become an import research issue. Studies demonstrated that mobile technology can aid or actively support collaboration [22].

Nevertheless, the idea of a collaborative learning game for mobile devices, specifically developed for the use in school classes, is a rather new one.

4 Concept and Design of the IPad App "Buchstaben Post"

TU Graz has been developing learning applications for iOS for several years, already starting in 2010. A number of workshops have been given on app design and how to achieve users' satisfaction [23].

Building on these insights, our goal was to develop an application for school children that makes use of personal devices in classrooms and combines the positive effects of cooperative peer learning and gamification.

4.1 Research Design

First we had to design and develop an appropriate application as well as a user interface for teachers. As a second step, the app had to be evaluated in a proper classroom setting. We conducted our first trials at two elementary schools in Graz.

The following pages will illustrate the idea and design of our app and provide a bit of technical background. Afterwards we will present and discuss the results of our evaluation.

4.2 Idea and Concept

"Buchstaben Post"[1] is primarily a learning game for schoolchildren between grades 1 to 4. The aim is to teach children the correct spelling of words with a focus on collaboration and communication between the players.

Our idea was the following: Connect up to four devices in a peer to peer session. While it is still possible to play alone, it is intended as a multiplayer game with 2 to 4 people. To achieve a level of cooperation, all players have to work together to progress to the next round. The teammates are supposed to sit on the same table. The tablets are placed beside or in front of each other, resembling the setting of a classical board game.

---

[1] https://itunes.apple.com/de/app/id736836885?mt=8.

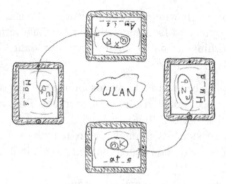

Fig. 1. Game setting

Many current learning games are too general regarding their content and lack a connection to curricula in school [24]. Thus, another important aspect was to provide teachers with the opportunity to create custom content for their children and to receive feedback. Especially school children in the first grades are only able to read or write a limited number of words, so the difficulty of the game had to be adjustable to fit the curriculum of the school class. For this purpose a user interface for teachers in form of a website had to be designed.

4.3   Technical Framework

We decided to use iOS as a platform for our application for two reasons:

1. TU Graz has a long history developing educational apps[2] for iOS.
2. Regarding tablets, iPads seem to be the preferred choice of schools.

"Buchstaben Post" is a native iOS application, for iPads only. As a programming language, Objective C was used.

The user interface for teachers was implemented in HTML and PHP, using a PHP framework called CodeIgniter.[3] MySQL was employed as database management system.

When developing software for children, special care has to be placed in designing the user interface of the application. Therefore, we took into consideration the iPad Human Interface Guidelines [25], as well as the extended guidelines focusing on mobile learning [26].

Establishing a peer to peer connection was another challenge, from the technical perspective as well as from a design point of view. The game was intended for school classes where each pupil is in possession of his own tablet device. We can assume that the children acquired a general proficiency in using the operating system. However, they will not have a concept of how a WLAN or Bluetooth connection works, or, for that matter, how the devices are connected at all.

---

[2] All apps are available at http://app.tugraz.at/.

[3] http://ellislab.com/codeigniter.

To address the problem, the application is able to connect over WLAN as well as Bluetooth. If one method is turned off or not able to establish a connection, the application will automatically try to connect over the other medium. Luckily, the iOS Gamekit framework supports that kind of connection management. Only the interface had to be adapted for the use of children.

4.4   Description of the IPad App

As mentioned before, the game can be played in single player mode. If that's the case, the goal of the game is simply to guess the correct spelling of a word. A hint in form of a sentence or a question and a number of letters are provided. The player has to substitute the missing letters of the word to guess. This is a well-known concept which already exists in numerous applications. Our idea was to use that approach and expand it in a way that would create a multiplayer application, where players not only had to guess their own words, but help each other out as well.

The game is not competitive, which means that the players are not "punished" for choosing a wrong letter, they can try as many times as they want. The game will not progress to the next round until all players have finished their words. Since it is meant to be played in a face-to-face setting, all players should be able to see the words of their teammates. Children who finish faster are thus able to help others out.

In order to further reinforce the idea of a "common goal", we provided another challenge for the players. While some players may possess all the missing letters of their word, other players will not be so lucky – they have to get the missing letters from one of their teammates.

The following section provides a more detailed explanation of the game mechanism.

4.5   The User Interface and Features

The application was originally developed for Austrian school classes. It is therefore only available in German language. However, the design of the app allows easy adaption to multilingual support in future versions.

The game is composed of four screens, not counting the splash (or loading) screen.

The figure on the left shows the start screen of the game. To keep it as simple as possible only two options are available. After choosing one, the player will be asked to sign in. This opens a login form, as depicted in the second figure (Fig. 2).

To log into the game, an account at the TU Graz user-management[4] system is required. While it is possible to play offline, the sign in is required for several reasons.

1. To download a custom list of words prepared by the teacher.
2. To store which words a player has already finished.

   Words are randomly drawn out of the assigned wordlist. However, words that have been selected once have a lower chance to appear again. Also, in order to ensure

---

[4] The user-management system will be explained in Sect. 4.3.

Fig. 2. Start screen   **Fig. 3.** Start screen with login form

that newly added content will not be omitted, "fresh" words have a much higher chance of being drawn.

3. To upload data of the children's performance.

   A learning application should offer feedback to the students as well as the teachers. While technically possible to store a multitude of data of the children's activity, it was hard to gather useful information for this particular setting. This is due to the fact that the game is highly cooperative and players are not able to complete a word without help of others. In the end, we decided to log the number of completed words for every pupil and the time it took for all players to finish one round.

The next two figures display the connection process. As depicted on Fig. 1, the players have two choices, either to start a new game (Fig. 3), or to join an already existing game (Figs. 4 and 5).

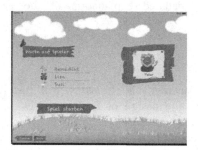

Fig. 4. Start game screen   **Fig. 5.** Join game screen

Both screens are designed in similar fashion. The first screen appears when a player opens a new game and shows the list of people which have already joined the game. The player who opened the game can decide to start it whenever he wishes. The "Join Game Screen" displays a list of open games. The player has to select one game and hit the "Join" button. Then he/she has to wait until the game is launched.

Fig. 6. Game screen

The next figure (Fig. 6) illustrates the main screen[5] of the app.

The middle of the screen contains the available letters (1), below, resting on the stone wall, is the word-to-guess (2). A hint for the word (3) is displayed in white letters above the middle section.

On the borders of the display, next to the railways, are the icons (4) of the team-mates located. These icons can be switched (by drag and drop), so that they reflect the sitting position of the players on table.

At the bottom left side are two buttons, "Return" and "Help", which are displayed in every screen except the first one. The "Return" button will end the game and take the player back to the start screen. The help button displays a help message in combination with arrows and images to further explain the gaming mechanism and functionality of the screen.

The first goal of the game is to fill in the missing letters of the incomplete word, by drag and dropping the letters into the right position. The second part is to help other players finish their words by sending them letters. To do that, the player has to drag the letter on one of the trains (5) or the area around. The icon (4) above the train represents the player the letter is sent to.

---

[5] Translation of the screen elements, from top to bottom: textfield (Nr. 3) „At this time of year it is very hot.", yellow railway signs "Send Letter", word-to-guess (Nr. 2) "Summer", button "Back", button "Help".

When all players have finished their words, a new round is initiated. The game server will semi-randomly draw words out of the downloaded word-pool (with priorities for new/unfinished words) and spread them among the players.

The game ends when there are no more words in the word-pool, or the player who launched the games closes it. If any of the other players leave, the missing letters will be spread among the reaming teammates and the game continues.

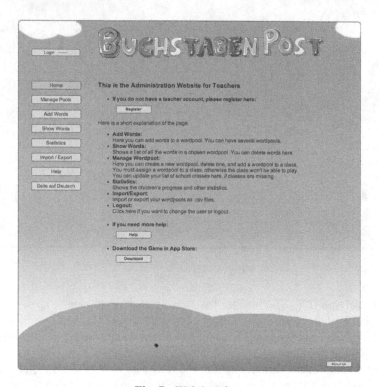

Fig. 7. Web-interface

4.6   Description of the Website for Teachers

The website[6] as shown in Fig. 7 is a simple interface for teachers to manage wordlists and receive feedback. To login, an account at the user-management system of the TU Graz is required. This is a database of local schools, containing accounts of teachers and pupils and their respective school classes. The system provides an interface for applications.

After a successful login, the teacher has several options. It is possible to create several wordlists, or "wordpools". Words can be constantly added or deleted from a pool. Afterwards the teacher has to assign a wordpool to a school class. In

---

[6] http://buchstabenpost.tugraz.at.

consequence, pupils who have logged in from the iPad application are able to play with the assigned pool.

In addition, teachers can export or import word-pools as.csv files. Another section of the website displays statistics of the children's performance, as mentioned before.

5 Using the App: Results and Discussion of the First Field Study

The first field study took place at two primary schools in Graz. Both schools have so called "iPad classes", in which every pupil is in possession of his/her own device. The first trial was performed at primary school Hirten, the second one at University of Teacher Education Styria. The field study took place in second grade classes, composed of 15 and 18 pupils. The children are used to working with the device and are proficient for their age. The trial was conducted as a participatory observation, followed by an interview with a group of children.

5.1 The Setting of the Field Study

The app was installed beforehand to save time. Every child had his own iPad. The players of each team were either sitting side by side or in front of each other. We decided to split the field study into two phases. First, the game was played in groups of two, afterwards in groups of four. Due to the nature of the game, a four player setting is more challenging and might have been too confusing for the beginning.

5.2 Results

The main part of our field study was the participatory observation. After a short explanation, the children were playing in groups of two for about 30 min, then in groups of four for the remaining part of the hour. The teacher and research assistant were helping out when they were stuck or had questions.

Here is an overview of the positive and negative aspects (in that order) of the test:

- The children quickly understood the concept of the game.
- While having some problems with the login and connection process, the game itself (game screen) was easy to use.
- There was steady communication between the players. This had been one of our main goals, but as a result the noise in the classroom was above the usual level, especially when the game was played in groups of four. While not necessarily negative, it is an aspect that has to be considered when employing the game.
- In almost every case, the children cooperated very well. When one player could not finish a word, he/she got help from his teammate. Or he/she tried to help his/her partner to finish his word and would then receive help himself. Some of the children were actively helping or grabbing letters by reaching out to their neighbor's iPad.
- The children generally seemed to enjoy the game and the resulting teamwork.

- They were motivated by finishing a word or round of the game.
- Sometimes words were challenging or unknown to the children or the hint or question was too vague. Yet they were very flexible in finding solutions, discussing among themselves and only asking for help when they could not reach a conclusion.
- Some groups were more competitive than others, trying to solve the puzzle as quickly as they could. One group even made a contest who could finish his/her word first.
- The main problem was of technical nature and appeared in form of connection failures as a result of establishing a connection over Bluetooth. The devices had both Bluetooth and WLAN activated (in case WLAN would not work due to network restrictions). In previous tests with only a limited number of devices (a maximum of four) these settings seemed to work well. Somehow, the Bluetooth framework appeared to be unable to cope with a multitude of connection requests, cancelling each other out. Disabling Bluetooth on all devices fixed the problem.
- The connection process posed some more difficulties. Due to the eagerness of the children to play, some of them were connecting to random players (instead of the one they were sitting next to), while others would not wait long enough for their partners to find the game or until it appeared in the in the list of available games (about 1-5 s delay). This, in combination with the technical problem mentioned above, lead to some confusion in the first minutes of the trial.
- As explained before, players have to sign in to receive custom wordlists. Filling in the correct password (a combination of letters and numbers, about 8-10 symbols long) was a challenge for some of the children, and they had to try several times.
- For a few pupils the difficulty was too high. They had trouble in reading and understanding the questions and spelling the words.
- In some cases children found it difficult to place the letter at the right position, because their dragging movement was not precise enough.

5.3 Results of the Interview

After observing the children's performance, a short interview with a handful of pupils, one of each group of players, was conducted. For this purpose, a number of questions and statements had been prepared. The children were asked to discuss the questions by themselves. Then, as a group, they had to show us if they agreed with a statement or not (by putting down smileys ranging from happy to sad). The prepared questions and answers are summed up in Table 1:

In case of question 2 and 4, the children were unsure and did not completely agree on an answer.

Afterwards, the children were asked to talk about their experiences with the game. The discussion affirmed the results of the observation, the children saying that they enjoyed playing together and had a lot fun. Some of them found the words a bit difficult. Among the most prominent statements were "We had fun" and "We would like to play some more". About a week after the test, further feedback was received

Table 1. Results of the interview

Question	Mean[a]
1. Did you like to play together?	1
2. Was the app easy to use?	1-2
3. Did you learn new words?	1
4. Was the difficulty of the game (words) ok?	1-3
5. Would you like to play again?	1

[a]"1" equals a very happy smiley, "5" a sad smiley.

from attending teacher, stating that the children chose to play "Buchstaben Post" (out of other learning games and activities) during their "free work time".

5.4   Children's Performance

As mentioned before, the app uploads data of the children's performance. The results will be discussed, however, it should be noted that those were only first trials of the app, focussed on the cooperative usage of the game, for insights on the learning efficiency, further studies have to be performed.

Analysis of the Data.   On average, it took the children about one and a half minute (92 s) to complete one round of the game. When playing in groups of two, it took them slightly less time (87 s) than in groups of four (100 s) – due to the fact that the missing letters are spread between more than one player in a game of four.

Figures 8 and 9 (Y-Axis: Time in seconds; X-Axis: Finished Rounds) illustrate the performance of the children (15 pupils) for the two parts of the test (groups of two and groups of four, 30 min for each part).

Figures 8 and 9 show the learning curves of the children. After 30 min of playing, they were significantly faster in completing one round of the game than in the beginning (on average), mainly due to two reasons:

- They were getting familiar with the game mechanisms.
- They were improving their teamwork over time.

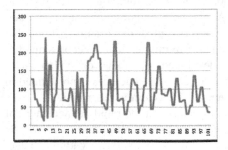

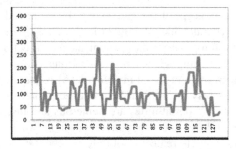

Fig. 8. Performance in groups of two   **Fig. 9.** Performance in groups of four

5.5 Summary of the Field Study

The research study is focussed on cooperation among peers and how to incorporate new technology and gaming into a classroom setting. Regarding this area of expertise, first field studies rendered practical feedback and the basis for further assumptions.

In summary it can be said that:

- The app fostered communication and collaboration.
- Given the right setting, children need little to no encouragement to support each other and work together.
- The presentation of learning content as a game is more enjoyable for children and motivates them to "play again".
- There are still a few technical difficulties that need to be addressed.

While the encountered problems were of minor nature and can easily be fixed, future work and more sophisticated studies need to be conducted regarding the learning results of the game compared to pure learning applications or traditional learning schemes. Furthermore a long-term study should be carried out to point out the improvement of learning results.

6 Conclusion

The project is focussed on cooperation among peers and how to incorporate new technology and gaming into a classroom setting. From our perspective, looking at the promising results of our first trials, the app successfully supported collaborative learning. Children are motivated to use this kind of application and they enjoy the resulting teamwork. The field studies rendered practical feedback and it can be stated that this study is a first step towards collaboration through mobile devices. Certainly, this field of research has much to offer. Regarding the project, several things come to mind: Further studies have to be performed, especially concerning the learning results of the application and how it compares to conventional learning methods.

Considering the social aspect, several questions arise: Does cooperation during the game affect the social behaviour in the classroom? Does it have a positive influence on the children and the class? Does it help them to work together in general, and not only when using the application?

From a technological point of view, the possibilities are numerous. To begin with, the concept of the game could be expanded. As the field study demonstrated, children very much like playing or learning together. Tablets or similar devices make it possible to sit together and communicate in a direct manner. Building on that concept, a number of learning games or applications could be developed that focus on collaborative learning and social interaction. Also, the number of connected devices is not limited in any way. It is possible to connect more or even all devices in a classroom.

The possibilities are numerous and fascinating and with the rapid advancement of mobile technologies, more and more ways to enhance the learning experience will be possible to realize - not only of school children, but for learners of every kind and age.

References

1. O'Reilly, T.: What is web 2.0?: design patterns and business models for the next generation software. Commun. Strat. **65**, 17–37 (2007)
2. Mann, B.D., Eidelson, B.M., Fukuchi, S.G., Nissman, S.A., Robertson, S., Jardins, L.: The development of an interactive game-based tool for learning surgical management algorithms via computer. Am. J. Surg. **183**(3), 305–308 (2002)
3. Johnson, D.W., Johnson, R.T.: An educational psychology success story: social interdependence theory and cooperative learning. Educ. Researcher **38**(5), 365–379 (2009)
4. Jordan, D.W., Le Métais, J.: Social skilling through cooperative learning. Educ. Res. **39**(1), 3–21 (2006)
5. Johnson, D.W., Johnson, R.T.: Making cooperative learning work. Theor. Pract. **38**(2), 67–73 (1999)
6. Holzinger, A.: Multimedia Basics. Volume 2: Cognitive Fundamentals of Multimedial Information Systems. New Delhi: Laxmi-Publications. Available in German by Vogel-Publishing (2002)
7. Dewey, J.: Democracy and Education: An introduction to the philosophy of education (Reprint 1997). Free Press, Rockland (1916)
8. Motschnig-Pitrik, R., Holzinger, A.: Student-centered teaching meets new media: concept and case study. IEEE J. Educ. Technol. Soc. **5**, 160–172 (2002)
9. Dillenbourg, P.: Collaborative Learning: Cognitive and Computational Approaches. Advances in Learning and Instruction Series. Elsevier Science Inc, New York (1999)
10. Chiu, M.M.: Group problem-solving process: social interactions and individual actions. J. Theor. Soc. Behav. **30**(1), 27–49 (2000)
11. Prince, M.: Does active learning work? Rev. Rese. J. Eng. Educ. **93**(3), 223–231 (2004)
12. Murphy, P.K., Wilkinson, I.A.G., Soter, A.O., Hennessey, M.N., Alexander, J.F.: Examining the effects of classroom discussion on students' comprehension of text: a meta-analysis. J. Educ. Psychol. **101**(3), 740–764 (2009)
13. Malone, T.W.: What makes things fun to learn? heuristics for designing instructional computer games. In: Proceedings of the 3rd ACM SIGSMALL Symposium and the 1st SIGPC Symposium on small systems, pp. 162–169 (1980)
14. Kafai, Y.B.: The Educational Potential of Electronic Games: From Games-To-Teach to Games-To-Learn
15. Papastergiou, M.: Digital game-based learning in high school computer science education: impact on educational effectiveness and student motivation. Comput. Educ. **52**(1), 1–12 (2009)
16. Zechner, J., Ebner, M.: Playing a game in civil engineering. In: 14th International Conference on Interactive Collaborative Learning (ICL2011) – 11th International Conference Virtual University (vu 2011), pp. 417–422 (2011)
17. Hannak, C., Pilz, M., Ebner, M.: Fun – a prerequisite for learning games. In: Proceedings of World Conference on Educational Multimedia, Hypermedia and Telecommunications 2012, AACE, Chesapeake, VA, pp. 1292–1299 (2012)
18. Ebner, M., Böckle, M., Schön, M.: Game based learning in secondary education: geographical knowledge of austria. In: World Conference on Educational Multimedia, Hypermedia and Telecommunications, pp. 1510–1515 (2011)
19. Ebner, M., Holzinger, A.: Successful implementation of user-centered game based learning in higher education: an example from civil engineering. Comput. Educ. **3**(49), 873–890 (2007)

20. Liang, J.K., Liu, T.C., Wang, H.Y., Chang, B., Deng, Y.C., Yang, J.C., Chou, C.Y., Ko, H.W., Yang, S., Chan, T.W.: A few design perspectives on one-on-one digital classroom environment. J. Comput. Assist. Learn. **21**(3), 181–189 (2005)
21. Kloper, E., Squire, K., Jenkins, H.: Environmental detectives: PDAs as a window into a virtual simulated world. In: Proceedings of the IEEE International Workshop on Wireless and Mobile Technologies in Education, pp. 95–98. IEEE Computer Society (2002)
22. Zurita, G., Nussbaum, M.: Computer supported collaborative learning using wirelessly interconnected handheld computers. Comput. Educ. **42**, 289–314 (2004)
23. Ebner, M., Kolbitsch, J., Stickel, C.: iPhone/iPad human interface design. In: Leitner, G., Hitz, M., Holzinger, A. (eds.) DASFAA 2014, Part I. LNCS, vol. 6389, pp. 489–492. Springer, Heidelberg (2010)
24. Egenfeldt-Nielson, S.: Beyond Edutainment: Exploring the Educational Potential of Computer Games, Ph.D. dissertation (2005)
25. iPad Human Interface Guidelines, (2010). http://itunes.tugraz.at/media/items/iphone_application_development-apple_ttt-2010-08/1281959367-hci_ipad.pdf
26. Huber, S., Ebner, M.: iPad human interface guidelines for m-learning. In: Berge, Z.L., Muilenburg, L.Y. (eds.) Handbook of mobile learning, pp. 318–328. Routledge, New York (2013)

Mining and Visualizing Usage of Educational Systems Using Linked Data

Selver Softic[1]([✉]), Behnam Taraghi[1], Martin Ebner[1], Laurens De Vocht[2],
Erik Mannens[2], and Rik Van de Walle[2]

[1] Department for Social Learning, Graz University of Technology- IICM,
Muenzgraben street 35A, 8010 Graz, Austria
{selver.softic,b.taraghi,martin.ebner}@tugraz.at,
http://www.tugraz.at
[2] iMinds - Multimedia Lab, Ghent University,
Gaston Crommelaan 8, 9000 Ghent, Belgium
{laurens.devocht,erik.mannens,rik.vandewalle}@ugent.be
http://www.ugent.be

Abstract. This work introduces a case study on usage of semantic context modelling and creation of Linked Data from logs in educational systems like a Personal Learning Environment (PLE) with focus on improvements and monitoring such systems, in generally, with respect to social, functional, user and activity centric level [7,15]. The case study demonstrates the application of semantic modelling of the activity context, from data collected over two years from the PLE at Graz University of Technology, using adequate domain ontologies, semantic technologies and visualization as reflection for potential technical and functional improvements. As it will be shown, this approach offers easy interfacing and extensibility on technological level and fast insight on statistical and preference trends for analytic tasks.

Keywords: Data mining · Linked data · Micro content · Education · Research

1 Introduction

Modern learning environments, beside learning resources provided by the educational institution, aim at integration of popular internet services that might be of interest of learners like: Google Hangout, Facebook, YouTube, Newsgroups, Twitter, Slideshare just to name some of them. Maintaining such platforms is intensively changing process demanding from maintainers to actively adapt their systems to the learner needs. Nowadays, learners are expecting focused and simple platforms helping them to organise their learning process. Learners don't want to waste their time on informations and actions which could disturb or prolong their learning. Therefore user adaptivity is a strong impact on acceptance of such platforms and should be matter of continuous improvement. Cumulated system monitoring data (e.g. logs) of such environments offers new

© Springer International Publishing Switzerland 2015
M. Ebner et al. (Eds): EiED 2014, CCIS 486, pp. 17–26, 2015.
DOI: 10.1007/978-3-319-22017-8_2

opportunities for optimization [13]. Such data can contribute the better personalization and adaptation of the learning process but also improve the design of learning interfaces. Main contribution of the paper is a case study done with the logs from PLE at Graz University of Technology presenting approach using Linked Data to mine the usage trends from PLE. The idea behind this effort is aiming at gaining insights [9] useful for optimization of PLE and adapting them to the learners by using more personalization e.g. through recommendation of interesting learning widgets.

2   Related Work

This section report shortly about most relevant related work regarding PLE (at Graz University of Technology) and semantic technologies used in this work.

2.1   Learning Analytics and Importance of Tracking and Reflection of User Logs

The current learning analytics research community defines [16] learning analytics as the analysis of communication logs [1,15], learning resources [11], learning management system logs as well existing learning designs [8,14] and the activity outside of the learning management systems [2,12]. The result of this analysis improves the creation of predictive models [6,18], recommendations [3,25] and refection [26]. Learning Analytics resides on algorithms, formulas, methods, and concepts that translate data into meaningful information. Modelling, structuring and processing the collected data derived from e.g. user behaviour tracking plays a decisive role for the evaluation. Different works outlined the importance of tracking activity data in Learning Management Systems [9,15,16,25,26]. None of them addressed the issue of intelligently structuring learner data in context and processing it to provide a flexible interface that ensures maximum benefit from collected information.

2.2   PLE at Graz University of Technology

The main idea of PLE at Graz University of Technology[1] is to integrate existing university services and resources with services and resources from the World Wide Web in one platform and in a personalized way [5,23]. The TU Graz PLE con- tains widgets [5,22,23] that represent the resources and services integrated from the World Wide Web. Web today provides lots of different services; each can be used as supplement for teaching and learning. The PLE has been redesigned in 2011, using metaphors such as apps and spaces for a better learner-centered application and higher attractiveness [4,21]. In order to enhance PLE in general and improve the usability as well as usefulness of each individual widget a tracking module was implemented by prior work [24] (Fig. 1).

---

[1] http://ple.tugraz.at.

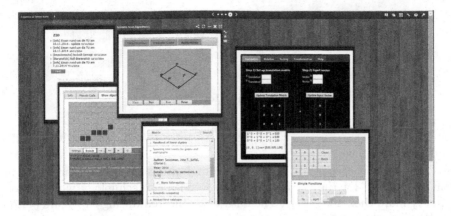

Fig. 1. PLE at Graz University of Technology

2.3   Semantic Modeling of Activities in PLE

The Semantic Web standards like RDF[2] and SPARQL[3] enable data to be and for interchange and queried as graphs. Data schema is usually projected on specific knowledge domain using adequate ontologies. This approach has been fairly successful used to generate correct interpretation of web tables [10] to advance the learning process [7, 13] as well to support the controlled knowledge generation in E-learning environments [20]. This potential was also recognised by resent research in *IntelLEO Project*[4]. *IntelLEO* delivered an ontology framework where *Activities Ontology*[5] is used to model learning activities and events related to them. Due to the relatedness to the problem that is addressed by this work this ontologies have been used to model the context of analytic data collected from PLE logs.

3   Approach for Mining Usage Logs

Presented approach is based on transforming collected data from PLE logs into instances of *Activities Ontology*. This process produces as output Linked Data graphs query able by SPARQL standard query language. The SPARQL is applied to query the Linked Data and mine the output for analytic visualizations (see Fig. 2). The overall goal of this processes is summarization, visualizations and evaluation of statistic data that enable the PLE optimization, in interface design and adaptation of content of PLE to the learner. This approach is inspired by the examples from current research in the area of Self-regulated Learners (SRL) [7, 19].

---

[2] http://www.w3.org/RDF.
[3] http://www.w3.org/TR/rdf-sparql-query/.
[4] http://intelleo.eu.
[5] http://www.intelleo.eu/ontologies/activities/spec/.

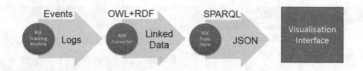

Fig. 2. Mining pipe line for PLE usage logs

3.1   Dataset

Data used in the case study originates from Personal Learning Environment (PLE) developed for the needs of Graz University of Technology which serves currently more then 4000 users. The data was collected during two years period in order to generate analytics reports with visualization support for overall usage and process view on our environment following the research trends of previous years [12, 17].

3.2   Modeling Usage Logs

The main precondition for meaningful mining of usage trends is choice of appropriate data model since RDF offers only the framework how structure and link data. This task concerns mostly the choice of the right vocabulary or ontology. *Activities Ontology* offers a vocabulary to represent different activities and events related to them inside of a learning environment with possibility to describe and reference the environment (in this case PLE) where these activities occur. Formulation in Listing 1.1 depicts an instance of usage AO:LOGGING instance. This excerpt comes from the tracking module. Such data is stored in a memory RDF Store (Graph Database for Linked Data) with SPARQL Endpoint (interface where Linked Data can be queried).This sample instance reflects that a usage AO:LOGGING event occurred at certain time point inside the learning widget named *LatexFormulaToPngWidget* as AO:ENVIROMENT. As shown in this example vocabularies and ontologies which suits well to specific case enriches the analytic process with a high level of expressiveness in a very compact manner.

3.3   Querying Usage Logs

Usage logs data presented as Linked Data graph are query able using SPARQL. In this way we are able to answer the questions like "Show me the top 15 used widgets?". Listing 1.2 represents exactly this question stated in the manner of SPARQL syntax.

4   Preliminary Results, Conclusion and Outlook

Advantages of Linked Data approach is usage of standardized web technologies which are scalable and flexible regarding the changes of representation structure

Listing 1.1. Sample model of a log for a PLE widget in N3 notation

```
@prefix ao: <http://intelleo.eu/ontologies/activities/ns/> .
@prefix rdf: <http://www.w3.org/1999/02/22−rdf−syntax−ns#> .
@prefix rdfs: <http://www.w3.org/2000/01/rdf−schema#> .

<http://ple.tugraz.at/ns/events/log/#7912>
    rdf:type ao:Logging;
    ao: occursIn <https://ple.tugraz.at/ns/widgets/#LatexFormulaToPngWidget>;
    ao:timestamp "2012−10−04T07:52:52" .

<https://ple.tugraz.at/ns/widgets/#LatexFormulaToPngWidget>
    rdf:type ao:Enivironment;
    rdfs:label "LaTeXFormulaPNG Converter" .
```

of data. Also very important aspect of mining PLE usage data using Linked Data is for sure high operational tolerance regarding incomplete analytic data instances as well as easier interfacing to other systems which could make use of information provided by PLE.

SPARQL as query language which operates over the Linked Data graphs of usage logs offers much flexibility regarding the generation of results, in different state of the art output formats, that should be visualized in end instance. It also allows on-demand statistical cumulations that can be used in the future as basic stats for recommendation of new widgets in the PLE or similar tasks.

Listing 1.2. Querying the intensity of usage of top 15 widgets in PLE.

```
PREFIX ao: <http://intelleo.eu/ontologies/activities/ns/> .
PREFIX rdf: <http://www.w3.org/1999/02/22−rdf−syntax−ns#> .
PREFIX rdfs: <http://www.w3.org/2000/01/rdf−schema#> .

SELECT DISTINCT ?widgetname ?date (COUNT(?widgetname) AS ?count)
WHERE
{
 ?x rdf:type ao:Logging;
    ao:occursIn ?widget;
    ao:timestamp ?date.

 ?widget rdf:type ao:Environment;
    rdfs:label ?widgetname.
}
GROUP BY ?widgetname
ORDER BY DESC(?count)
LIMIT 15
```

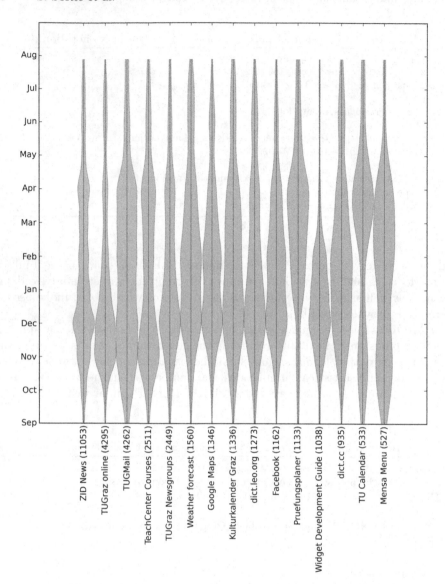

Fig. 3. Top 15 activities for an academic year time period 2011-2012

As preliminary result presented approach allows us mining the trends of PLE widgets usage overall time periods like presented in Fig. 3. This violin graph depicts the visual answer of the query from Listing 1.2. Also the intensity shows that as expected that most activity on widgets happens at the beginning when PLE is presented in introductory lectures to the newcomers and freshmen and at the end of academic terms when most of the students prepare for examinations. The statistics visualisation help us to gain deep insight into the behaviour of a users in a certain period of time. Presented approach generates uniform interfaces

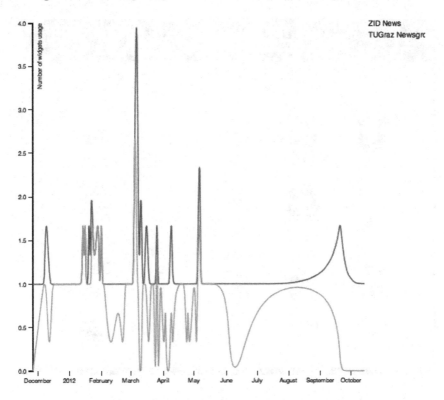

ZID News
TUGraz Newsgr

Fig. 4. Comparision of two news widgets.

for information exchange, enables flexibility for visual analytics, and also includes the flexibility regarding the enrichment of learning analytics data with Linked Data sources from the Web. The spread of applicability covers wide range of analytics methodologies like prediction, reflection and as result of these the intervention field. Figure 4 reflects the advantage of such approach where e.g. two widgets with similar purpose can be visually compared (in this case two newsgroups widgets). Future efforts regarding improvement semantic structure data layer, besides the mentioned Linked Data could also include precisely defined categorisation, userwise statistics of learning widgets, since PLE can also provide this information. Especially the learning widget store as part of PLE could profit from this improvement. Mostly used and favored widgets by users will be ranked higher and recommended by the store itself as shown in Fig. 5. By tracking the usages on user level the teachers will be able to draw conclusions about the popularity and quality of their learning widgets.

The overview over distribution of usage logs can reflect the overall interest of the users within PLE. Such inputs evaluated and interpreted in appropriate way contribute implicitly the improvement of the quality of services for students and teachers. The PLE becomes, in technical manner, extensible and well connected by standardized and intelligent interfaces and available for other web based tools and services.

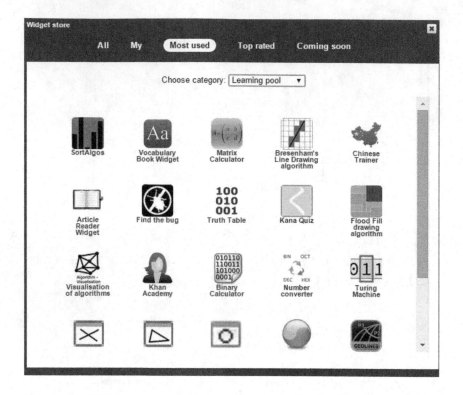

Fig. 5. PLE Widget store recommendations based upon usage log statistics.

Acknowledgements. The research activities that have been described in this paper were funded by Graz University of Technology, Ghent University, iMinds (an independent research institute founded by the Flemish government to stimulate ICT innovation), the Institute for the Promotion of Innovation by Science and Technology in Flanders (IWT), the Fund for Scientific Research-Flanders (FWO-Flanders), and the European Union.

References

1. Bakharia, A., Dawson, S.: Snapp: a bird's-eye view of temporal participant interaction. In: Proceedings of the 1st International Conference on Learning Analytics and Knowledge, pp. 168–173. LAK 2011, ACM, New York, NY, USA (2011). http:// doi.acm.org/10.1145/2090116.2090144
2. Blikstein, P.: Using learning analytics to assess students' behavior in open-ended programming tasks. In: Proceedings of the 1st International Conference on Learning Analytics and Knowledge, pp. 110–116. LAK 2011, ACM, New York, NY, USA (2011). http://doi.acm.org/10.1145/2090116.2090132

3. Drachsler, H., Bogers, T., Vuorikari, R., Verbert, K., Duval, E., Manouselis, N., Beham, G., Lindstaedt, S., Stern, H., Friedrich, M., Wolpers, M.: Issues and considerations regarding sharable data sets for recommender systems in technology enhanced learning. Procedia Comput. Sci. **1**(2), 2849–2858 (2010). http://www.sciencedirect.com/science/article/pii/S1877050910003236, proceedings of the 1st Workshop on Recommender Systems for Technology Enhanced Learning (RecSysTEL 2010)

4. Ebner, M., Scerbakov, N., Taraghi, B., Nagler, W., Kamrat, I.: Teaching and learning in higher education an integral approach. In: Gibson, D., Dodge, B. (eds.) Proceedings of Society for Information Technology and Teacher Education International Conference 2010, pp. 428–436. AACE, San Diego (2010). http://www.editlib.org/p/33375

5. Ebner, M., Taraghi, B.: Personal learning environment for higher education-a first prototype. In: World Conference on Educational Multimedia, Hypermedia and Telecommunications, pp. 1158–1166 (2010)

6. Fancsali, S.E.: Variable construction for predictive and causal modeling of online education data. In: Proceedings of the 1st International Conference on Learning Analytics and Knowledge, pp. 54–63. LAK 2011, ACM, New York, NY, USA (2011). http://doi.acm.org/10.1145/2090116.2090123

7. Jeremić, Z., Jovanović, J., Gašević, D.: Personal learning environments on the social semantic web. Semant. Web **2**(12), 8–12 (2012)

8. Lockyer, L., Dawson, S.: Learning designs and learning analytics. In: Proceedings of the 1st International Conference on Learning Analytics and Knowledge, pp. 153–156. LAK 2011, ACM, New York, NY, USA (2011). http://doi.acm.org/10.1145/2090116.2090140

9. Mazza, R., Milani, C.: Exploring usage analysis in learning systems: gaining insights from visualisations. In: Workshop on Usage Analysis in Learning Systems, Proceedings of Artificial Intelligence in Education. Amsterdam (2005)

10. Mulwad, V., Finin, T., Syed, Z., Joshi, A.: Using linked data to interpret tables. In: Proceedings of the the First International Workshop on Consuming Linked Data, November 2010

11. Niemann, K., Schmitz, H.C., Scheffel, M., Wolpers, M.: Usage contexts for object similarity: exploratory investigations. In: Proceedings of the 1st International Conference on Learning Analytics and Knowledge, pp. 81–85. LAK 2011, ACM, New York, NY, USA (2011). http://doi.acm.org/10.1145/2090116.2090127

12. Pardo, A., Kloos, C.D.: Stepping out of the box: towards analytics outside the learning management system. In: Proceedings of the 1st International Conference on Learning Analytics and Knowledge, pp. 163–167. LAK 2011, ACM, New York, NY, USA (2011). http://doi.acm.org/10.1145/2090116.2090142

13. Prinsloo, P., Slade, S., Galpin, F.: Learning analytics: challenges, paradoxes and opportunities for mega open distance learning institutions. In: Proceedings of the 2nd International Conference on Learning Analytics and Knowledge, pp. 130–133. LAK 2012, ACM, New York, NY, USA (2012). http://doi.acm.org/10.1145/2330601.2330635

14. Richards, G., DeVries, I.: Revisiting formative evaluation: dynamic monitoring for the improvement of learning activity design and delivery. In: Proceedings of the 1st International Conference on Learning Analytics and Knowledge, pp. 157–162. LAK 2011, ACM, New York, NY, USA (2011). http://doi.acm.org/10.1145/2090116.2090141

15. Rosen, D., Miagkikh, V., Suthers, D.: Social and semantic network analysis of chat logs. In: Proceedings of the 1st International Conference on Learning Analytics and Knowledge, pp. 134–139. LAK 2011, ACM, New York, NY, USA (2011). http://doi.acm.org/10.1145/2090116.2090137

16. Santos, J.L., Govaerts, S., Verbert, K., Duval, E.: Goal-oriented visualizations of activity tracking: a case study with engineering students. In: Proceedings of the 2nd International Conference on Learning Analytics and Knowledge, pp. 143–152. LAK 2012, ACM, New York, NY, USA (2012). http://doi.acm.org/10.1145/2330601.2330639

17. Santos Odriozola, J.L., Verbert, K., Govaerts, S., Duval, E.: Visualizing PLE usage. In: Proceedings of EFEPLE11 1st Workshop on Exploring the Fitness and Evolvability of Personal Learning Environments, pp. 34–38. CEUR WS, Aug 2011. https://lirias.kuleuven.be/handle/123456789/322006

18. Sharkey, M.: Academic analytics landscape at the university of phoenix. In: Proceedings of the 1st International Conference on Learning Analytics and Knowledge, pp. 122–126. LAK 2011, ACM, New York, NY, USA (2011). http://doi.acm.org/10.1145/2090116.2090135

19. Siadaty, M., Jovanovic, J., Pata, K., Holocher-Ertl, T., Gasevic, D., Milikic, N.: A semantic web-enabled tool for self-regulated learning in the workplace. In: ICALT, pp. 66–70. IEEE Computer Society (2011). http://dblp.uni-trier.de/db/conf/icalt/icalt2011.html#SiadatyJPHGM11

20. Softic, S., Taraghi, B., Halb, W.: Weaving social e-learning platforms into the web of linked data. In: I-Semantics, pp. 559–567 (2009)

21. Taraghi, B., Ebner, M., Clemens, K.: Personal learning environment - generation 2.0. In: World Conference on Educational Multimedia, Hypermedia and Telecommunications, pp. 1828–1835. AACE (2012)

22. Taraghi, B., Ebner, M., Schaffert, S.: Personal learning environments for higher education: a mashup based widget concept. In: Proceedings of the Second International Workshop on Mashup Personal Learning Environments (MUPPLE 2009), Nice, France, pp. 1613–0073 (2009)

23. Taraghi, B., Ebner, M., Till, G., Mühlburger, H.: Personal learning environment-a conceptual study. iJET Int. J. Emerg. Technol. Learn. 5(S1), 25–30 (2010)

24. Taraghi, B., Stickel, C., Ebner, M.: Survival of the fittest - utilization of natural selection mechanisms for improving ple. In: Proceedings of the First Workshop on Exploring the Fitness and Evolvability of Personal Learning Environments, pp. 4–9 (2011)

25. Verbert, K., Drachsler, H., Manouselis, N., Wolpers, M., Vuorikari, R., Duval, E.: Dataset-driven research for improving recommender systems for learning. In: Proceedings of the 1st International Conference on Learning Analytics and Knowledge, pp. 44–53. LAK 2011, ACM, New York, NY, USA (2011). http://doi.acm.org/10.1145/2090116.2090122

26. Verbert, K., Manouselis, N., Drachsler, H., Duval, E.: Dataset-driven research to support learning and knowledge analytics. Educ. Technol. Soc. 15(3), 133–148 (2012)

Determining the Causing Factors of Errors for Multiplication Problems

Behnam Taraghi[1]([✉]), Matthias Frey[1], Anna Saranti[1], Martin Ebner[1],
Vinzent Müller[2], and Arndt Großmann[2]

[1] Graz University of Technology, Münzgrabenstrasse 35/I, 8010 Graz, Austria
{b.taraghi,martin.ebner}@tugraz.at
{s0473056,freym}@sbox.tugraz.at
[2] UnlockYourBrain GmbH, Französische Str. 24, 10117 Berlin, Germany
{vinzent.mueller,arndt}@unlockyourbrain.com

Abstract. Literature in the area of psychology and education provides domain knowledge to learning applications. This work detects the difficulty levels within a set of multiplication problems and analyses the dataset on different error types as described and determined in several pedagogical surveys and investigations. Our research sheds light to the impact of each error type in simple multiplication problems and the evolution of error rates for different error types in relation to the increasing problem-size.

Keywords: Learning analytics · Multiplication · Math · Education · Error types

1 Introduction

Learning simple multiplications is one of the major goals in the first years at primary school education. Math teachers find pedagogically relevant to know which exercises improve mathematical abilities, which errors occur repeatedly and on which steps they may require teacher's intervention. Applying math training applications can support the teachers in this regard and enhance the basic math education at primary schools [1]. For example, the 1×1 trainer application [2] that was first developed by Graz University of Technology, assists the training process of pupils and enhances the pedagogical intervention of the teachers for learning one-digit multiplication problems at schools. The application was used in several primary schools for training goals. In our previous works [3,4] we analysed the gathered data (about 500,000 calculations) to get insight about the learners' answering behaviour within this application. We identified difficulty levels within the set of one-digit multiplication problems. In this work we continue our research on another dataset generated by the Android application *UnlockYourBrain*[1], which poses different basic mathematical questions to the learners. The focus is drawn first to the multiplication problems.

---

[1] http://unlockyourbrain.com/en/.

© Springer International Publishing Switzerland 2015
M. Ebner et al. (Eds): EiED 2014, CCIS 486, pp. 27–38, 2015.
DOI: 10.1007/978-3-319-22017-8_3

We perform the same analysis steps as in our previous work to identify the difficulty levels. We primarily want to shed light to the reasons of the incorrect answers. Therefore, based on the error rates driven from the first part of the analysis, for each multiplication problem we detect different error types known from the literature. We present the probabilities of occurrence of the various error types in detail and explain them individually, for each specific multiplication problem.

Section 2 describes the dataset that is used for analysis purposes. Section 3 covers the difficulty levels of the multiplication problems, the findings and interpretations based on the difficulty probabilities. Section 4 describes the analysis of the detected error types leading to the conclusion and future work in Sect. 5.

1.1 Related Work

There are two major arithmetic models of fact retrieval that deal with errors in simple multiplications; the modified network interference theory by Campbell [5] and the interacting neighbours model by Verguts and Fias [6]. Both models introduce some common error types and their cause in simple multiplication problems.

One of the most occurring error types in simple multiplication problems are the *operand errors*. They happen whenever the failed result is the product of one of the neighbouring operands instead of the given ones; e.g. 48 = **6** * 8 for the given problem **7** * 8. The survey done by Campbell [5], shows that the majority of errors can be classified in this category. The operand error rates differ for each multiplication problem and are not uniformly distributed [7].

Operand intrusion error happens when at least one of the two operands matches one of the digits of the result; e.g. answering **7**4 to the posed question **7** * 8. Campbell argued that reading the operands as if they were two-digit numbers causes this error. This argument is supported from the fact that the first operand is observed in the decade digit's place and/or the second operand appears at the unit digit of the result [7,8].

One of the initial findings in solving arithmetic problems is the so called problem-size effect. The problem size is defined as the sum of the operands [9]. The error rates increase as the problems get larger and the response time evolve correspondingly. The only exceptions are *Five problems* (problems involving 5 as operand e.g. 5 * 7) and *tie problems* (problems with repeated operands e.g. 4 * 4), that do not exhibit this error to a large extend. These problems can be answered faster in comparison to other problems of the same category [10].

The interacting neighbour model of Verguts and Fias [11] introduces the concept of consistency of multiplication problems. The concept of consistency was formerly known from the language literature [12], where it was proposed that the reaction time to pronounce a given word depends on the consistency of the word to its neighbours, with respect to pronunciation. In the context of simple multiplications, each problem has a set of *neighbouring* problems. The operands that are used in these problems, are the neighbours of the operands (in the multiplication table) of the original problem. Two arbitrary problems are consistent if their solutions have the same decade or unit digits; e.g. $5\underline{6} = 7 * 8$ and $3\underline{6} = 4 * 9$ are two consistent problems with respect to their unit digit. The authors argue, that the consistency measure explains the problem-size effect as well as the tie effect. Tie problems have less neighbours and they are inconsistent rather than consistent. Hence less competition exists for tie problems. For all *five problems* there are consistent neighbours with distance 2 (they share 5 as unit digit). Although the neighbour distance is far, it is assumed to be the reason for smaller error rates. Altogether, multiplication problems that have a higher consistency with their neighbours can be answered faster with higher accuracy [13].

2   Dataset Description

The learning application that was used to provide insight for the characterisation of learning difficulties is *UnlockYourBrain*. Android users are confronted with basic mathematical questions each time they attempt to unlock their screen. The application provides for each posed question a list of possible answers; only one of them is correct. The list has variable length, meaning that it can vary from trial to trial between two and five possible answers, even if the posed question is the same. The answering process evolves as follows: the learner can either attempt to answer or chooses to skip the usage and continue with unlocking the screen. In case of an answering attempt, either the correct answer is chosen and the application finishes, or a wrong answer is selected. In the latter case the application indicates the mistake and repeats the question with the remaining possible answers. The user reattempts to answer the question with less possible answers or chooses to skip.

The dataset was cleaned to remove noise and was reduced to a minimum number of occurrences of entities in order to ensure a high degree of confidence in the statistical results. The methods used can be read at [14]. The final dataset contained 268 questions that were posed totally 1191450 times to 46357 users.

3   Answer Types and Difficulty Levels
of Multiplication Problems

A measure of the difficulty of a question is the answering manner of the learners. The possible answer types are gathered in the following set {R, WR, W, WWR, WW, WWWR, WWW, WWWW} where W means "wrong" and R "right". A question that was posed with three answering options (see [14]) can have three answering types: R which denotes that the user found the correct answer in the first answering attempt, WR that the first attempt was wrong but the second right and WW that both attempts failed. The set of answer types is the classification algorithm's dimensions. Every multiplication lies in an eight-dimensional feature space where the value in each dimension is the probability that the question was answered as the corresponding answer type. By applying the K-Means algorithm [15] in this space we classified the problems in 11 clusters; each of them contains problems that were answered in similar means from the learners.

Figure 1 depicts the computed difficulty probabilities (error rates) of all provided multiplication problems within the dataset. A low probability indicates a rather easy problem whereas a high probability implies a relatively difficult one.

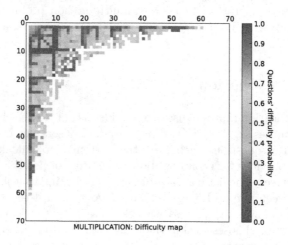

Fig. 1. Difficulty map of multiplication problems. Axes stand for the two operands A and B of a multiplication problem $A * B$. Low probabilities imply lower error rates, hence rather easy problems. High probabilities indicate relatively difficult problems.

It can be observed that the difficulty values appear to a great extent symmetric. The error rate of problems $A * B$ and $B * A$ seem to be strongly correlated, therefore the order of operands probably does not have a decisive influence on the error rate. One-digit multiplication problems are considered easier than the two-digit multiplications. Looking further into the set of one-digit multiplications (the top left quadratic area in Fig. 1 where both operands are less than ten) we achieve the same results as we gained in our previous research work [3] in the one-digit multiplication problems. *5* and *10 problems* are relatively easier to solve. The problems involving operands 6, 7, 8 and 9 are rather difficult problems.

Looking into two-digit problems, we observe the influence of the 5 and 10 operands in the simplicity of the question containing them. As in one-digit problems, the unit digits 1, 2 and 5 show the lowest error rates. The same is true for *difficult operands*. It can be seen that specially the unit digits 6, 7 and 8 make the two-digit problems extremely difficult relative to the other operands. Considering the problems containing 5 as unit digit, the combination with *difficult operands* as decade digit leads to a higher error rate, compared to the other decade operands.

The *tie effect* is also visible. The problems containing repeated operands have lower error rates compared with other neighbour problems, but the problem-size must be also taken into account. While the tie problems in the interval of one-digit problems are relatively easy, they become more difficult for two-digit problems. The provided dataset in our case contains tie problems no greater than $17 * 17$. In Fig. 1, problems $11 * 11$ and $12 * 12$ seem easy due to their unit digits (1 and 2 effect); $15 * 15$ shows relatively a lower rate than the other tie problems with operands greater than $12 * 12$. It can be argued that the use of 5 as one of the operands could explain this phenomenon.

4   Analysis of Error Types

The complete list of analysed error types with a short explanation can be found in Table 1. For a sample given multiplication problem $56 = 7 * 8$ an example is given to clarify how to interpret an error type. For instance, a given answer 48 to the sample problem $7 * 8$ is associated with the error type *operand error split 1*. 48 is the correct answer to the multiplication problem $\underline{6} * 8$, which in turn is the product of the neighbouring operand $\underline{6}$ in the multiplication table with distance 1, hence *operand error split 1*.

4.1   Operand Errors

The majority of errors can be categorized as operand errors. The operand error rates differ for different multiplication problems (see Sect. 1.1). Figure 2 depicts the probabilities of an *operand error* for each simple multiplication problem where each square represents a specific problem. The first operand can be read off the X-axis, the second operand off the Y-axis. The color of the square indicates the probability of an *operand error* occurrence for the corresponding problem; red color indicates higher probabilities and blue color a very low probability. As it can be seen, the problems that are rather difficult (see Sect. 3) are more affected by operand errors than the easy ones.

Figures 2a and b show the probabilities of an *operand error* with the split of 1 and 2. Comparing the two heatmaps, it is visible that the shortest neighbour distance (split 1) contains the most operand errors; e.g. for a given problem $\underline{7} * 8$ the errors such as $48 = \underline{6} * 8$ are more probable than $40 = \underline{5} * 8$. It is observable that the most difficult problems have the highest operand error rates. Relatively easy problems comprised by operands 2, 5 and 10 show the lowest error rates. This is also true for operand errors with split 2. One can verify that the error rates are also not uniformly distributed over all problems. *Five problems* are less affected from the effects that were described above. We can observe a slightly higher error rate for *five problems* that involve an operand greater than 5 though. It can be argued that the *difficult operands* account for this effect.

Table 1. The analysed error types and their descriptions.

Error type	Description	e.g. $56 = 7 * 8$
operand errors	a neighbouring operand is taken	
split 1	the neighbouring distance is 1	$48 = \underline{\mathbf{6}} * 8$
split 2	the neighbouring distance is 2 for an operand or is 1 for both operands	$40 = \underline{\mathbf{5}} * 8$
which operand?	is the smaller or the larger operand affected? Ties were ignored	
which neighbours?	are smaller or larger neighbours taken?	
operand intrusions	a digit of the result matches an operand	
first operand	decade digit matches first operand	$\underline{\mathbf{7}}4 \hookleftarrow \underline{\mathbf{7}} * 8$
second operand	unit digit matches second operand	$6\underline{\mathbf{8}} \hookleftarrow 7 * \underline{\mathbf{8}}$
consistency errors	only one digit is correct	
unit consistency	only unit digit is correct	$7\underline{\mathbf{6}} \hookleftarrow 5\underline{\mathbf{6}}$
decade consistency	only decade digit is correct	$\underline{\mathbf{5}}1 \hookleftarrow \underline{\mathbf{5}}6$
off errors	result differs by $\pm x$ at most	
off-by-one	the result differs by ± 1	55 or 57
off-by-two	the result differs by ± 2 at most	$54, 55, 57, 58$

Looking further into operand errors with split 1, that account for the majority of errors, it can be observed that the larger operand neighbours are more frequently responsible for the cause of errors than the smaller ones. In other words, learners tend to choose a value greater than the true result of a problem rather a decremented one; e.g. for a given problem $4 * \underline{\mathbf{8}}$ the errors such as $36 = 4 * \underline{\mathbf{9}}$ are more probable than $28 = 4 * \underline{\mathbf{7}}$. Figures 2c and 2d show this finding. We emphasize that this is a valid prediction for all simple multiplications. Looking further through each multiplication individually, we observe some exceptions such as $9 * 7$ and $7 * 9$ where a decremented operand is rather due. Furthermore the *tie problems* seem to follow the same rule as can be seen in Fig. 2d.

Considering the operand errors with split 1 and incremented operands, the next step was to analyse which operand accounts for the error. More specifically, to investigate which one is incremented: the larger or the smaller operand. Our analysis shows that the mean probabilities for the set of larger and smaller operands are extremely close to each other, so that we can not claim that the relative size of operands plays an important role. Figures 2e and 2f show this comparison for each multiplication problem. As an example it can be seen that $8 * 4$ or $4 * 8$ show a very high error rate, meaning that the most probable false answer in this case was $36 = \underline{\mathbf{9}} * 4$.

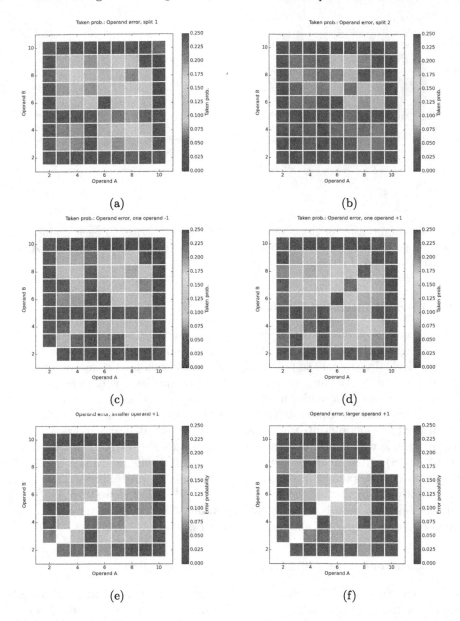

Fig. 2. Probabilities (error rates) of an *operand error* for each simple multiplication problem. Figures 2a and b compare the error rates of an *operand error* with the split of 1 and 2 respectively. Figures 2c and d depict errors with *decremented* and *incremented* operands, respectively. These are restricted to the error rates of operand errors with a split of 1. Figures 2e and f compare errors caused by *smaller* and *larger* operands respectively. These are restricted to the error rates of operand errors with a split of 1 incremented.

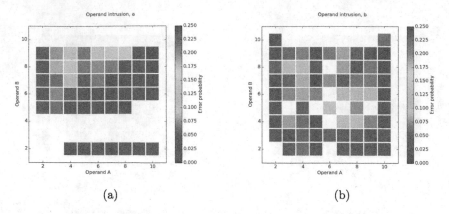

(a)   (b)

Fig. 3. Probabilities (error rates) of an *operand intrusion error* for each simple multiplication problem. Figures 3a and b show the error rates for the first operand A and the second operand B respectively.

4.2 Operand Intrusions Errors

Operand intrusion errors occur when an operand intrudes into the result. Figure 3 depicts the error rates for the first operand A and the second operand B respectively. In general the probability of an intrusion for the second operand B is higher than for the first operand A. While no specific pattern can be found within the set of simple multiplication problems, it can be observed that some operands reveal a higher probability relatively to other problems. For instance in case of the first operand intrusion, specially the operand $A = 4$ shows a probability over 10 % while multiplied by difficult operands $B \in \{7, 8, 9\}$. Interestingly $A \in \{4, 6, 7, 8\}$ are more often intruded to the results while multiplied by $B = 9$. In case of second operand intrusion, $B = 6$ reveals a probability of 12 % while being multiplied by difficult operands $A \in \{7, 8, 9\}$. It is followed by $A \in \{3, 4\}$ multiplied by $B = 8$. In both cases, first operands $A \in \{6, 7, 8, 9\}$ play a stronger role in operand intrusion compared with other operands.

4.3 Consistency and Off Errors

Considering the decade and unit consistency errors, we could find no clear pattern in the multiplication table. The probability of error occurrence related to decade consistency is relatively higher than unit consistency. Decade consistency errors are more probable if both operands are different and greater than 5. This observation can be explained by the problem-size effect.

Bearing in mind that the decade consistency errors include failed results that differ by a constant distance, it is interesting to explore how far this distance is. Figure 4 depicts the *off-error* rates. These are associated with the failed answers that differ form the correct answer by a constant number x. The most observed

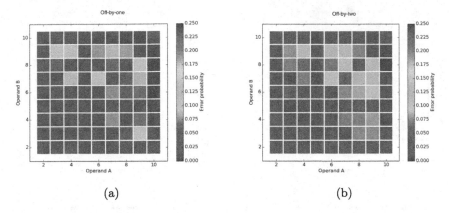

Fig. 4. Probabilities (error rates) of *off errors* for each simple multiplication problem. Figures 4a and 4b show the off-by-one and off-by-two error rates respectively.

off-errors lay between ± 2. As depicted in Fig. 4 the off-by-one and off-by-two errors occur merely for difficult problems that were identified in Sect. 3.

4.4 Problem Size Effect

Problem-size is the sum of the operands and expresses how large the problem is. Figure 5a shows the error rate (of any type) against increasing problem size. As the problem size increases, the error rate has also a tendency to increase. However there is no continuous ascending course of error rate. As predicted in [5, 7, 10] the tie problems can be answered faster and more accurate compared with other problems, also while the problem size increases. We see here that the tie problems have a different course by ascending problem-size. While the error rates for all other error types increases, in tie problems a decrease is observed. This can be claimed only upto problem size 25, due to the fact that the provided dataset for the analysis is restricted. Furthermore, the error rates for the tie problems have a local minimum at $5 * 5$, $10 * 10$ and $15 * 15$, which can be argued by the 5 effect and the easy 10-problems.

We analysed each error type described in Table 1 against the problem size individually. Decade and unit consistency errors increase by ascending problem-size. Figures 5b and c depict the unit and decade consistency errors against problem size respectively. All other analysed error types do not reveal any increasing course and stay constant within a close probability interval. As an example, the operand error with split 1 is depicted against the problem size in Fig. 5d. It can be observed that the error rate varies between 5 % and 10 % and comes even down to about 3 % at problem size 25. In sum, considering the set of analysed error types, the problem-size effect can be defined according to the unit and decade consistency errors.

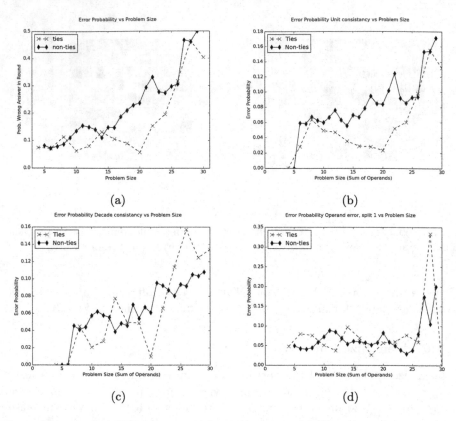

Fig. 5. Error probabilities (fraction of errors) against problem size. Problem size is calculated as the sum of the operands $A + B$. The largest considered operand is 15. Ties and non-ties are depicted separately. Figure 5a shows the general round error probability; that is the fraction of rounds where at least one error of any type has been made against problem size. Figure 5b depicts the unit consistency errors and Fig. 5c shows the decade consistency errors against the problem size.

5   Conclusion and Future Work

In this work we analysed the multiplication problems and explored the difficulty levels. We concluded that the order of the operands does not play a role in the difficulty of the problem. One-digit problems involving operands 6, 7, 8 and 9 are rather difficult problems. Concerning two-digit problems, we observed that the unit digits 1, 2 and 5 show the lowest error rates as in one-digit problems. Considering the problems containing 5 as unit digit, the combination with difficult operands as decade digit leads to a higher error rate, compared to the other decade operands.

Looking further into the incorrect answers we analysed different error types known from the literature. The majority of errors could be categorized as operand errors. Generally the problems that are rather difficult are more affected by operand errors. The shortest neighbour distance (split 1) contains the most operand errors, as expected. Additionally the larger operand neighbours are more frequently responsible for the cause of errors than the smaller ones.

Finally, we analysed the effect of ascending problem size on different error types. We could show that there is no continuous ascending course of error rate while the problem size increases. Furthermore the error rates for *tie problems* follow a very different course compared to other problems. While the error rates for all other error types increases, in tie problems a decrease can be observed. Due to the fact that the provided dataset was restricted, these findings can be claimed only upto problem size 25.

Considering the course of each analysed error type individually (in relation to increasing problem size), we could observe an increasing error rate only for consistency errors. All other analysed error types do not reveal any increasing course and stay constant within a close probability interval. Consequently considering the set of analysed error types, the problem-size effect can be defined according to the unit and decade consistency errors.

Until now, questions were characterised by their relative difficulty. A classification according to the error types that are observed would be more informative. The detection of new types of errors in other basic mathematical operations is an ongoing work. The main interests are not only in the field of one-digit operations but also extending to two-digit operations, which are arguably less analysed [16]. The determination of error types and the probability of their occurrence for each learner is the first step to the creation of a student model that grasps the misconceptions of basic mathematical operations.

References

1. Ebner, M., Schön, M.: Why learning analytics in primary education matters. In: Karagiannidis, C., Graf, S. (eds.) Bulletin of the Technical Committee on Learning Technology, vol. 15, Issue 2, pp. 14–17 (2013)
2. Schön, M., Ebner, M., Kothmeier, G.: It's just about learning the multiplication table. In: Shum, S.B., Gasevic, D., Rebecca, F. (eds.) Proceedings of the 2nd International Conference on Learning Analytics and Knowledge (LAK 2012), pp. 73–81. ACM, New York, NY, USA (2012). DOI=10.1145/2330601.2330624
3. Taraghi, B., Ebner, M., Saranti, A., Schön, M.: On using markov chain to evidence the learning structures and difficulty levels of one digit multiplication. In: Proceedings of the 4th International Conference on Learning Analytics and Knowledge, pp. 68–72, Indianapolis, USA (2014)
4. Taraghi, B., Saranti, A., Ebner, M., Schön, M.: Markov chain and classification of difficulty levels enhances the learning path in one digit multiplication. In: Zaphiris, P., Ioannou, A. (eds.) LCT 2014, Part I. LNCS, vol. 8523, pp. 322–333. Springer, Heidelberg (2014)
5. Campbell, J.I.D.: Mechanisms of simple addition and multiplication: a modified network-interference theory and simulation. Math. Cognit. **1**, 121–165 (1995)
6. Verguts, T., Fias, W.: Interacting neighbours: a connectionist model of retrieval in single-digit multiplication. Mem. Cognit. **33**, 1–16 (2005)

7. Campbell, J.I.D.: On the relation between skilled performance of simple division and multiplication. J. Exp. Psychol.: Learn. Mem. Cognit. **23**, 1140–1159 (1997)
8. Campbell, J.I.D., Clark, J.M.: Cognitive number processing: an encoding-complex perspective. In: Campbell, J.I.D. (ed.) The Nature and Origins of Mathematical Skills, pp. 457–491. Elsevier Science, Amsterdam (1992)
9. Zbrodoff, N.J., Logan, G.D.: What everyone finds: the problem size effect. In: Campbell, J.I.D. (ed.) Handbook of Mathematical Cognition, pp. 331–346. Psychology Press, New York (2004)
10. LeFevre, J.A., Sadesky, G.S., Bisanz, J.: Selection of procedures in mental addition: reassessing the problem size effect in adults. J. Exp. Psychol.: Learn. Mem. Cognit. **22**, 216–230 (1996)
11. Verguts, T., Fias, W.: Neighborhood effects in mental arithmetic. Psychol. Sci. **47**, 132–140 (2005)
12. Seidenberg, M.S., McClelland, J.L.: A distributed, developmental model of word recognition and naming. Psychol. Rev. **96**, 523–568 (1989)
13. Domahs, F., Delazer, M., Nuerk, H.: What makes multiplication facts difficult: problem-size or neighborhood consistency? Exp. Psychol. **53**, 275–282 (2006). doi:10.1027/1618-3169.53.4.275
14. Taraghi, B., Saranti, A., Ebner, M., Müller, V., Großmann, A.: Towards a learning-aware application guided by hierarchical classification of learner profiles. J. Univ. Comput. Sci. Special Issue on Learning Analytics (2015). http://www.jucs.org/jucs_21_1/towards_a_learning_aware
15. Bishop, C.: Pattern Recognition and Machine Learning, pp. 424–430. Springer Science and Business Media, LLC, New York (2006)
16. Nuerk, H.C., Moeller, K., Klein, E., Willmes, K., Fischer, M.H.: Extending the mental number line, a review of multi-digit number processing. J. Psychol. **219**(1), 3–22 (2011)

Tutoring Teachers - Building an Online Tutoring Platform for the Teacher Community

Sten Govaerts[1], Yiwei Cao[2(✉)], Nils Faltin[2],
Faysal Cherradi[2], and Denis Gillet[1]

[1] EPFL, Lausanne, Switzerland
{sten.govaerts,denis.gillet}@epfl.ch
[2] IMC AG, Saarbrücken, Germany
{yiwei.cao,nils.faltin,faysal.cherradi}@im-c.de

Abstract. Knowledge sharing has been a trendy and recurring topic in technology-enhanced learning for years. Many advanced platforms have been developed. However face-to-face help session are still often preferred by people who want to enhance their skills. The Go-Lab project aims to engage school students with STEM topics by bringing online laboratory experiments into the classroom. To achieve this, teachers are the key to success. Accordingly, the teacher's knowledge and skills in inquiry learning with online labs are important, since it may be a hurdle for teachers to use such technical software and apply it in their lessons. To support and tutor teachers with this, we have developed the Go-Lab Tutoring Platform that offers teachers a peer assistance and expertise sharing platform. Teachers, lab owners, and pedagogical experts can help each other and share their skills and knowledge. To sustain this tutoring platform, we aim to set up a business model to support the community build-up in a sustainable way. This paper elaborates on the design, the first prototype and an early evaluation of the Go-Lab Tutoring Platform.

Keywords: Online labs · Inquiry learning · Tutoring · STEM · Social tutoring platform · Teacher professional development · Community building · Business model

1 Introduction

In our ever-changing world, technology is evolving at a very fast pace, both on the hardware / software and connectivity levels. Children start using smart phones and tablets at a younger and younger age and technology is penetrating more schools. This requires more adaptation and continuous training for teachers who use technology in the classroom. Bringing technology-enhanced science, technology, engineering, and mathematics (STEM) learning into the schools, is what the European Go-Lab project[1] is set out to do by integrating exciting online laboratory experiments into the courses to encourage students to study

---

[1] The Go-Lab project, http://www.go-lab-project.eu.

© Springer International Publishing Switzerland 2015
M. Ebner et al. (Eds): EiED 2014, CCIS 486, pp. 39–51, 2015.
DOI: 10.1007/978-3-319-22017-8_4

STEM. Teachers can create such learning activities with online labs by using the Go-Lab Portal[2]. Through this portal, teachers can find online labs and the necessary resources to build their inquiry activities and use online laboratories in the classroom straight from the browser with no setup cost [9,10].

Online labs and inquiry learning methods enable school students' creativity for science learning and bring them engagement and fun [11,12]. Such online labs can also be much more convenient than setting up physical experiments in the classroom itself. It can even bring experiments that would be impossible to conduct before, to the students. For instance, through the Go-Lab Portal teachers and students can operate the high-powered, robotic Faulkes telescope[3] located in Hawaii from the classroom to investigate astronomy, or students can investigate particle collisions using real data from the CERN Large Hadron Collider [13].

However, both students and teachers need to learn how to conduct inquiry learning with online labs. Teachers are key to bring this technology into the classroom, since they teach the students. Besides their conventional professional development, teachers are also required to master more ICT skills [1,2], e.g. to use the Go-Lab Portal and operate online labs. To overcome these barriers, the Go-Lab project provides a platform for peer assistance and tutoring teachers on how to use online labs and appropriate pedagogical methodologies. Knowledge sharing practices are considered important factors for learning by many educators [7,17]. Moreover, an inquiry learning case study shows that the teacher's expertise influences the success of their students greatly [3]. Thus, training teachers can be a very effective means to support students learning STEM.

The Go-Lab Tutoring Platform offers teachers assistance from lab owners, scientists and their peers who can share their expertise and experience with online labs, pedagogy and the Go-Lab Portal. For instance, a tutor can offer a help session on how to use an online lab or how to create an inquiry activity. After teachers have become more experienced, they can peer assist other teachers.

Thanks to the American *No Child Left Behind Act*, the US Department of Education pays the tutoring bills. In the European Go-Lab project, we are investigating incentives for experts and teachers to provide tutoring sessions in a sustainable way. To assess the usability and preferences towards such incentives, we have conducted two evaluations with 14 teachers and 7 researchers (the latter evaluation was already reported in [4]). The Go-Lab Tutoring Platform shows the potential to make teacher training scalable and sustainable.

First, this paper presents related online assistance platforms. After which we elaborate on our design and implementation. Then, the evaluations with teachers and researchers are presented and incentive mechanisms are discussed to sustain the tutoring platform. Finally, we conclude with our future plans.

2   Related Work

This section first surveys existing tutoring platforms with their business models and afterwards incentives to offer tutoring are discussed.

---

[2] The Go-Lab Portal, http://www.golabz.eu.
[3] The Faulkes Telescope Project, http://faulkes-telescope.com/.

The market for tutoring will boom according to the Global Industry Analysts (GIA) who predicts the global private tutoring market surpasses over 100 billion dollar by 2018[4] as private tutoring will be accepted by more and more students. *Tutor.com* with over 2500 online tutors is popular in the USA and charges monthly membership fees. This business model is also applied to the similar platforms *studyedge.com* and *instaEDU.com*. The latter also provides tutoring for Massive Open Online Courses (MOOC) [15]. *takelessons.com* offers tutoring services paid by attending local or online courses.

Specific teacher-focused tutoring platforms aim at teachers' professional development. *teacherspayteachers.com* is a marketplace for teachers to share lesson plans for free or by payment. *lessoncast.com* offers a free and paid membership and teachers can share their teaching resources, get coaching, and attend online professional development courses. Teachers are motivated to win the digital badges thanks to their collaboration with the Digital Innovation in Learning Awards.[5] These platforms are aimed at the American K12 teacher communities. Similarly, teacher tutoring has great potential as well. Many teachers invest time in attending courses & workshops (71 % of teachers), and conferences & seminars (44 % of teachers) for professional development [16].

There are also general-purpose tutoring platforms targeting all users. *Google Helpouts*[6] integrates the Google Hangouts video chatting functionality to offer free or paid help sessions with experts (e.g. in cooking or repairing your computer). Their business model is offering paid video consulting sessions of which Google retains a 20 % fee and pays the instructor 80 %. At its initial launch, Google manually selects experts for quality assurance. Amazon's *Mayday*[7] offers live tech support to Amazon customers. The development of tutoring platforms is more active in the USA than Europe. However, the European School Net offers the *eTwinning platform*[8] [6], where European teachers are able to collaborate and share teaching resources for free.

Second, different credit systems are surveyed to explore how the Go-Lab Tutoring Platform could evaluate and award teachers and tutors. For example, social media techniques (e.g. badges, ratings, comments, or credits) can highlight skills, achievements, or the engagement of an individual in online platforms [8].

The *Mozilla OpenBadges* platform[9] develops the Open Badges standard for online assessment. By collecting widely-accepted, portable Open Badges, learners keep motivation high to study. Social help platforms, such as the Q&A site StackExchange[10], often use social rating mechanisms to rate questions, answers and the authors. Limpens et al. [14] proposed a competence model using a decentralised virtual currency system as an incentive for self-regulated learner

---

[4] Forbes article, http://www.forbes.com/sites/jamesmarshallcrotty/2012/10/30/global-private-tutoring-market-will-surpass-102-billion-by-2018/.

[5] dila 2014, http://awards.edsurge.com/.

[6] Google Helpouts, https://helpouts.google.com.

[7] Amazon Mayday, http://amazon.com/maydaytv.

[8] eTwinning, http://www.etwinning.net/.

[9] Mozilla Open Badges, http://openbadges.org/.

[10] StackExchange, http://stackexchange.com/.

communities. Similarly, with *Credly*[11] user can earn Credly credits in various platforms, such as Facebook, Twitter and Moodle.

Chang et al. [5] use such ratings to compute an overall trust score of a tutor's expertise, which is often an extra incentive to these tutors. But even digital badges with their different granularity and different ways to obtain are deemed valuable by users [8]. Such decentralized credit granting can be useful for adult learning or professional development, as shown in EDUCAUSE that issues digital badges to recognise professional ICT achievements in higher education[12]. eTwinning assigns quality labels at national and European levels to motivate teachers to participate in more European teaching projects. However these badges are not portable to other platforms. Class Badge[13] is a free online platform for teachers to award students with badges.

Based on this state of the art, the Go-Lab Tutoring Platform aims to build a teachers' community for online labs and inquiry learning activities. It tackles the potential business model and employment of a credit system.

3   Realisation of the Go-Lab Tutoring Platform

This section presents the requirements analysis, architecture and the user interface of the Go-Lab Tutoring Platform.

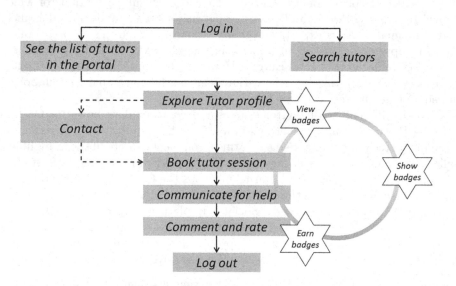

Fig. 1. Workflow in the Go-Lab tutoring platform

---

[11] Credly, https://credly.com/.

[12] EDUCAUSE, https://www.educause.edu/.

[13] Class Badge http://classbadges.com/.

3.1   Requirements

Based on user scenarios we conducted a requirement analysis for Go-Lab Tutoring Platform (more details are in [4]).

The main functionality for novice teachers, who are looking for help, is summarised in Fig. 1. Imagine a novice teacher looking for help to use online labs in her class, she logs in, searches for tutors and explores several tutor profiles, books a session, communicates for help during the session, and comments and rates the tutor after the session. Such comments, ratings and digital badges may play a role to help novice teachers to find a trustworthy tutor. After a succefully completed help session, both the teacher and tutor can award each other badges, comments and ratings that are shown on their profile.

3.2   Architecture of the Go-Lab Tutoring Platform

Figure 2 depicts the architecture of the Go-Lab Tutoring Platform and its relationship to the Go-Lab Portal and Booking System. The Go-Lab Tutoring Platform is supported by a credit system and a set of components to find and book tutors. The social platform components manage user and tutor profiles and provide social features such as user comments and ratings on the user profiles and the help sessions. Users can write comments related to the help session and rate the help sessions and the tutor using a five star rating on each other's profile. The average rating is calculated and listed in each user profile. The contact & communication component provides different contact channels between users and tutors. Such channels are required for communication and to conduct the help session. They comprise emails, contact forms, chat rooms, screen-sharing, and video-chatting. For example, one can email a tutor to make an appointment, while the help session itself is done through the video chatting tool.

Users can book a help session with a tutor via the tutor booking component, which supports calendar-based booking through the Go-Lab booking system.

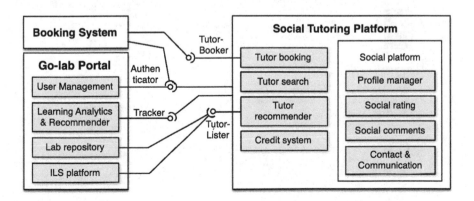

Fig. 2. The architecture of the Go-Lab Tutoring Platform

Users can search for tutors via the tutor search component and get recommendations of tutors on the portal through the tutor recommender component and the tutor search interface. The credit system provides mechanisms (digital badges) to award tutors for the provided help.

3.3   User Interface

The Go-Lab Tutoring Platform is accessible at http://tutoring.golabz.eu and implemented with Drupal 7. Figure 3 depicts the home page with user login information on right upper corner. The main top menu allows access to the user's profile, her calendar and booked session, which shows notifications of new actions that occurred since the last login. Those new actions can be:

- *As a tutor:* my help sessions that have been booked by other users.
- *As a tutor:* my booked help sessions that have been cancelled.
- *As a user:* my booked help sessions that have been cancelled by the tutor.

The search box in Fig. 3 enables search through both profiles and help offers of tutors. In the search results, each tutor with their name, ranking, and profile is listed, similarly as in Fig. 3 which is before the filtering.

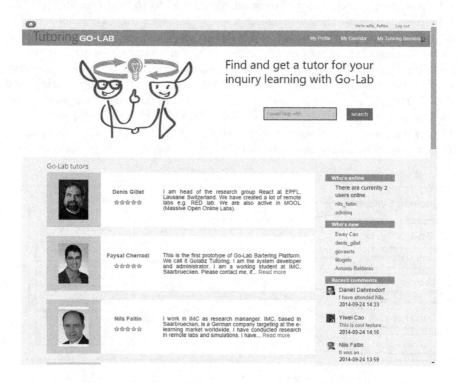

Fig. 3. Home page of the Go-Lab Tutoring Platform

When users come to the Go-Lab Tutoring Platform, they are required to register and login, either with their Google account or they can create a new account in the Go-Lab Tutoring Platform. Without login, they can only view tutor information but they are not allowed to create or book any help session.

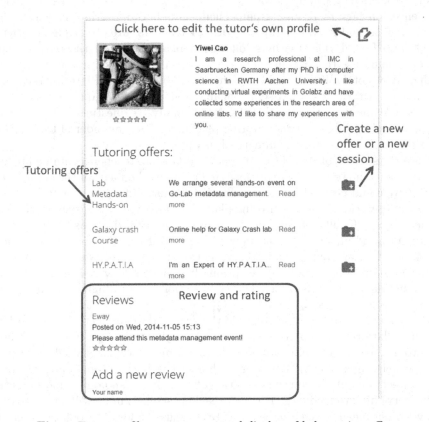

Fig. 4. Tutor profile management and display of help session offers

Each tutor's profile is managed on the platform as depicted in Fig. 4. It displays a basic description of the tutor with contact information and average ratings as well as labs and inquiry spaces in which the tutor has expertise. A tutor can list the help sessions she offers, which can be booked. Tutors have access to a centralised booking calendar, 'My calendar', by clicking the booking button on the upper-right corner. Users can comment and rate this tutor. The profile rating will be calculated as an average. More advanced and robust rating metrics can be considered when needed.

4   Evaluation

To evaluate the usability and usefulness of the platform, two user studies have been conducted. Apart from usability and usefulness assessment, participatory design (PD) activities were conducted to assess preferences of teachers to guide our design. The first survey was conducted with 7 PhD students at the JTEL Summer School 2014. The students acted both as teachers and experts and offered and received help using the prototype. In this first survey, we enquired about the users' skills and knowledge about physical and online labs, and their preferences on how to receive experts' help and the appropriate incentives for tutors. The second survey was done with 14 teachers already acquainted with the Go-Lab Portal. The teachers followed a presentation of the purpose and how they could use the system. This format was chosen because the survey was conducted remotely. They could use the Go-Lab Tutoring Platform but were not obliged. Afterwards, we assessed again their preferences on the delivery of help and the incentives to provide help. Additionally, we questioned the usability and perceived usefulness of the tutoring platform. The remainder of this section elaborates on the results as summarised in Fig. 5.

Both the surveys of the JTEL students and Go-Lab teachers contained recurring questions, however some questions differ due to the focus of the survey and the fact we could get real teacher feedback. The usability (question 4 & 6) and usefulness (question 5) of the tutoring platform prototype was surveyed with the teachers. The difficulty of the functionality was perceived as easy to very easy (question 6) and almost all teachers would not need technical assistance (question 4, low median, but spread). The functionality features were perceived as useful (question 5, high median). Additionally, teachers provided suggestions for other functionality such as Google Docs integration, a multilingual user interface, and a Frequently-Asked-Questions (FAQ) section.

Using participatory design to guide the future developments of the Go-Lab Tutoring Platform, the participants were asked about their preferences on how they would like to get help (question 1) and which incentives would motivate them to help (question 2). Question 1 shows that both students and teachers prefer direct communication such as face-to-face help (a) and online meetings (b) (both (very) high to medians). However teachers seem to more willing to look for help via other means, such as a helpdesk (c), discussion fora (d), online search (f) and even social media (e) is liked by many. While the JTEL students prefer these solutions less (lower medians) and are less aligned about these (larger spread). Some teachers also provided other channels they would like to use, namely help videos (*'videos help a lot, we see someone using what we have to learn how to use and learn without effort.'*), webinars (*'also useful webinars or hangouts on air'*), email exchange (*'Why don't we have personal e-mail exchanges with a PPT/prezi attachments. ... And what is the most important - you know who uses the platform you stay in close contact with a group of people. Teachers like writing messages, share ideas.'*) and FAQ (*'Maybe some questions that may be recurring, can integrate a FAQ page for each specific lab/apps.'*).

The incentives that motivate people to help each other (question 2) seem to lean towards getting something in return, whether it is social media badges (high median), other tutoring session (preferred more by teachers than students), or financial incentives (high median). Giving tutoring for free was perceived a bit

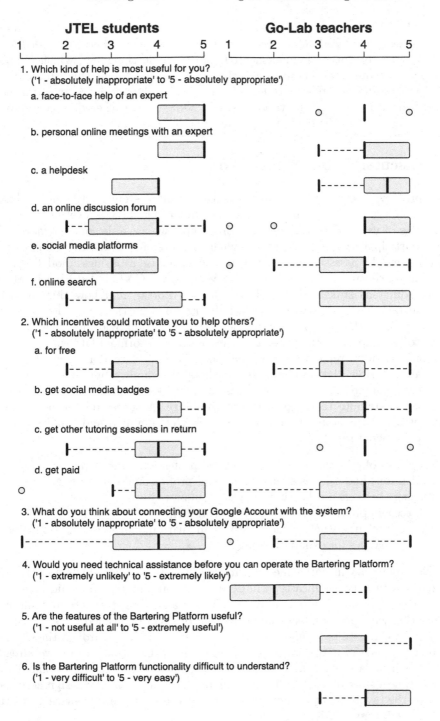

Fig. 5. Boxplots of the likert scales of the survey with JTEL students and Go-Lab teachers.

better by the teachers than the students. One teacher even said *'People LOVE meeting people, a face to face occasion is a wonderful way of sharing enthusiasm.'*

Since the prototype is implemented using Google Hangouts, which requires a Google account, we enquired whether participants found this problematic. However, most teachers and students did not object. Furthermore, most teachers have been using Google to various extent. Only one teacher does not have a Google account, but is ready to apply for one if necessary.

5   Discussion and Future Work

The prototype has been launched, but the credit system is still under development. Currently, only the rating and commenting show a level of trust and expertise of users. However, with the prototype, we are able conduct more concrete participatory design workshops where the preferences of novice and expert teachers can be assessed (see Sect. 4) to conceptualise a business model.

The conceptual diagram in Fig. 6 shows how the Go-Lab Tutoring Platform affects different stakeholders and the Go-Lab Portal, and how this can lead to a sustainable business model. Go-Lab organises participatory design workshops with teachers who evaluate the platform and provide feedback that is used to develop the next version of the Go-Lab Tutoring Platform. The help sessions are often related to user scenarios of the Go-Lab Portal. For this, the Go-Lab Tutoring Platform supports teachers' community building and professional development. Such training sessions and events have business potential and can contribute to the project sustainability. A successful business model will sustain both the platform and the teacher community, and could be based on the following resources:

- Ministries of education sponsor teachers' professional development.
- Institutions and schools sponsor teachers' professional development.
- Teachers help each other and earn some money.
- Lab owners promote their labs by offering help.
- Amateur scientists help novice teachers and earn money, but can also be interested in paying for expert tutoring.

Non-monetary incentive mechanisms (e.g. (portable) digital badges and well-recognised teacher certificates) will be used in conjunction with paid offers. To make the professional development certificates a success story support and collaboration with policy makers and organisations will be needed.

Go-Lab aims to build and support a teacher community through the Go-Lab Tutoring Platform and the Portal. Within the Go-Lab consortium, we already have teachers, lab owners and a school who promotes teachers' professional development, as a start of this effort. Furthermore, the participatory design activities lead to the involvement of more teachers and the iterative improvement of the Go-Lab Tutoring Platform in the future.

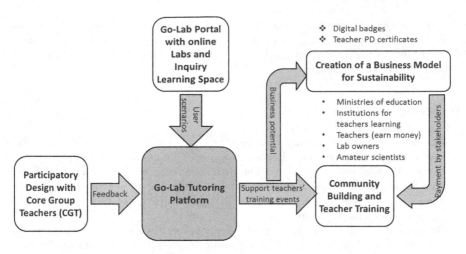

Fig. 6. Conceptual diagram leading towards a business model

6   Conclusion

Nowadays, teachers are life-long learners that continuously need to keep up with the latest technological and pedagogical innovations. We have created a peer assistance and tutoring platform for teachers who want to apply online labs and inquiry learning methods in STEM. The Go-Lab Tutoring Platform has multiple goals. First, it offers an effective community-building tool for teachers and experts to share and exchange their teaching expertise and knowledge. Second, it supports a dynamic professional development path for novice teachers who can through peer tutoring become expert teachers. Third, the potential business model can enable the Go-Lab Tutoring Platform and Portal to become a sustainable marketplace for knowledge and skill sharing on online labs and pedagogy. Finally, the Go-Lab Tutoring Platform serves as a support mechanism for the Go-Lab Portal by providing tutoring activities that can attract more teachers.

The evaluation results of the prototype prove the concept as a promising solution to support teachers with bringing online labs into the classroom. Through this evaluation, we have investigated incentives to motivate teachers and tutors, which provides an indication for a potential business model to involve diverse stakeholders: ministries of educations, teacher professional development organisations, teachers, and amateur scientists. In the future, we aim to improve the usability, include incentives, a credit system and other interesting features requested in the evaluation, as well as work on building up a STEM teacher community for online labs and inquiry learning.

Acknowledgments. This research work is partially funded by the European Union in the context of the Go-Lab project (Grant Agreement no. 317601) under the Information and Communication Technologies (ICT) theme of the 7th Framework Programme for

R&D (FP7). This document does not represent the opinion of the European Union, and the European Union is not responsible for any use that might be made of its content. We would like to thank Matthias Heintz and Effie L.-C. Law (University of Leicester) for their teacher survey support.

References

1. Education and training; supporting teacher competence development - for better learning outcomes. Technical Report, European Commission, July 2013
2. Breuer, R., Klamma, R., Cao, Y., Vuorikari, R.: Social network analysis of 45,000 schools: a case study of technology enhanced learning in europe. In: Cress, U., Dimitrova, V., Specht, M. (eds.) EC-TEL 2009. LNCS, vol. 5794, pp. 166–180. Springer, Heidelberg (2009)
3. Brinkerhoff, J., Glazewski, K.: Support of expert and novice teachers within a technology enhanced problem-based learning unit: a case study. Int. J. Learn. Technol. **1**(2), 219–230 (2004)
4. Cao, Y., Govaerts, S., Dikke, D., Faltin, N., Gillet, D.: Helping each other teach: design and realisation of a social tutoring platform. Journal of Immersive Education (JiED) (to appear)
5. Chang, H.H., Chuang, S.S.: Social capital and individual motivations on knowledge sharing: Participant involvement as a moderator. Inf. Manage. **48**(1), 9–18 (2011)
6. Crawley, C., Gilleran, A., Scimeca, S., Vuorikari, R., Wastiau, P.: Beyond school projects, a report on etwinning 2008–2009. Technical Report, Central Support Service for eTwinning (CSS), European Schoolnet (2009)
7. Dewey, J.: Experience and Education. The Kappa Delta Pi lecture series. Simon and Schuster, New York (1997). http://books.google.de/books?id=UWbuAAAAMAAJ
8. Finkelstein, J., Knight, E., Manning, S.: The potential and value of using digital badges for adult learners. Technical Report American Institutes for Research (2013)
9. Gillet, D., de Jong, T., Sotirou, S., Salzmann, C.: Personalised Learning Spaces and federated online labs for STEM education at school: supporting teacher communities and inquiry learning. In: Proceedings of the 4th IEEE Global Engineering Education Conference (EDUCON), pp. 769–773. IEEE (2013)
10. Govaerts, S., Cao, Y., Vozniuk, A., Holzer, A., Zutin, D.G., Ruiz, E.S.C., Bollen, L., Manske, S., Faltin, N., Salzmann, C., Tsourlidaki, E., Gillet, D.: Towards an online lab portal for inquiry-based STEM learning at school. In: Wang, J.-F., Lau, R. (eds.) ICWL 2013. LNCS, vol. 8167, pp. 244–253. Springer, Heidelberg (2013)
11. de Jong, T., Linn, M.C., Zacharia, Z.C.: Physical and virtual laboratories in science and engineering education: review. Science **340**(6130), 305–308 (2013)
12. de Jong, T., Sotiriou, S., Gillet, D.: Innovations in STEM education: the go-lab federation of online labs. Smart Learn. Environ. **1**(3), 1–6 (2014)
13. Kourkoumelis, C., Vourakis, S.: Hypatia - an online tool for ATLAS event visualization. Phys. Educ. **49**(1), 21–32 (2014)
14. Limpens, F., Gillet, D.: A competence bartering platform for learners. In: Leung, H., Popescu, E., Cao, Y., Lau, R.W.H., Nejdl, W. (eds.) ICWL 2011. LNCS, vol. 7048, pp. 148–153. Springer, Heidelberg (2011)
15. McAuley, A., Stewart, B., Siemens, G., Cormier, D.: The MOOC model for digital practice (2010)

16. OECD: TALIS 2013 Results: An International Perspective on Teaching and Learning. OECD Publishing (2014). http://www.oecd-ilibrary.org/education/talis-2013-results_9789264196261-en
17. Wenger, E.: Communities of practice - Learning, Meaning, and Identity. University Press, Cambridge (1998). http://www.ewenger.com/theory/index.htm

Towards Digital Immersive and Seamless Language Learning

Thomas Strasser[⊠] and Wolfgang Greller

University of Teacher Education Vienna, Vienna, Austria
{thomas.strasser,wolfgang.greller}@phwien.ac.at

Abstract. Modern technologies facilitate new forms of learning. Technology-enhanced language learning (TELL) has seen dramatic changes in the facilitation of self-directed learning opportunities, but also in enhancing the learning experience in classroom-based formal language learning. In our study, we investigate the potential of new technologies and want to find out how immersion teaching is supported through seamless learning approaches.

Keywords: Immersion · Seamless language learning · CLIL · e-Portfolios · Technology-enhanced learning · Formal learning · Informal learning · Mobile learning · Smartphones

1 Introduction and Concepts

Immersion is one of the key pedagogic concepts in language teaching [1]. The idea behind immersion teaching is to embed learners in a linguistic and cultural environment that is equivalent to that of a native speaker, thus facilitating acquisition of the foreign or second language (FL, L2) in a simulated mother tongue (L1) situation. This method stands beside other more traditional language teaching approaches that focus on the acquisition of linguistic concepts and competences (grammatical, communicative, etc.). Historically, language immersion can be traced back to the post-WWII days with the establishment of Ulpan courses in Israel that aimed to teach Hebrew to new immigrants. In these settings, students were instructed in the Hebrew language and culture for better integration. The idea was taken up in other countries, and, by the mid-1980s, language immersion had developed a strong foothold in various bilingual communities and in the teaching of lesser-used languages in Wales, Quebec, Brittany, and elsewhere [2]. Primarily adult-oriented in the outset, the high motivation and intensity of the approach led to successful learning outcomes and a positive perception by language learners [3]. More recently, the approach has been transferred and somewhat modified to cover 'content and language integrated learning' (CLIL) in general foreign language classes. Here, certain subject disciplines are taught in the target language to facilitate not only FL learning but also subject knowledge and competences [4]. Still, despite large similarities, there are also important differences between immersion and CLIL [5].

In technology-enhanced learning (TEL), immersion takes a somewhat different perspective and mainly refers to the perceived technology-facilitated environment, such as 3D worlds, games or ambient learning displays [6, 7]. In this short paper, we propose

M. Ebner et al. (Eds): EiED 2014, CCIS 486, pp. 52–62, 2015.
DOI: 10.1007/978-3-319-22017-8_5

to merge the two concepts into a seamless language learning experience and to use modern learning technologies to simulate a situated native environment for immersion.

Seamless learning can be described in a multitude of ways. Conceptualisations and definitions vary from 'the seamless integration of technologies into classrooms [...]' to marking 'the border between formal and informal learning or individual and social learning' [8]. Other experts define seamless learning as 'learning wherever, whenever and whatever' [9].

In principle, we see three main bridging functions in seamlessness: (1) formal – informal; (2) across devices and applications; (3) blended learning, i.e. scenarios spanning online and offline episodes of learning (cf. [10]). Taking the conceptual and terminological versatility of seamless learning into consideration, a certain consensual approach in the scholarly literature can be noted, though: common to most definitions is the aim to support continuous, fluid learning experiences – mainly driven by the learner's desire to inquire or to investigate. The concept of seamless learning is to make the transitions between the different learning situations and context as smooth as possible [11].

The question arises how technology can make a language learning experience fluid and student-centred, focusing on learning/teaching designs that span different activities and contexts. The following chapter seeks to investigate formal and informal learning contexts (mainly at tertiary level), their applicative scenarios and consecutively their conceptual proximity to seamless learning.

2 Formal/Informal Learning and Its Relation to Seamless Learning

There is little doubt that technological innovations like the Internet have initiated a vivid discussion concerning the reformation or adaptation of higher education in general [12–16]:

Higher education is a dynamic, complex system embedded in an even more dynamic and complex supersystem - human society. Technological innovations have radically changed this supersystem [...] [17].

However, Wiley [17] suggests that especially technological developments have often not been didactically implemented in tertiary education curricula:

While commercial industries have converted these technological advances into consumer benefits, thereby making customers happier and improving their own financial bottom lines, higher education has largely ignored these changes in its supersystem.

In his paper, Wiley explicitly emphasises a certain shift concerning learning techniques in the digital age from formal, institution-based education to everyday or informal learning (learning in extra-curricular settings [13]). In general, Wiley argues that formal learning within an institutionalised context (seen from a learning-theoretical point of view) is something analogue, tethered, isolated, generic, consumption-oriented and closed, whereas informal learning (e.g. situated, ubiquitous and extra-curricular learning) focuses on digital, mobile, connected, personal, constructivist and open learning performances and therefore pays conceptual attention to the technological developments of the 21st century.

Informal or everyday learning within a digital context is frequently carried out with mobile devices such as the smartphone or a tablet-PC [14, 18, 19]. In order to establish a holistic, fluid and 'seamless' learning approach, it is of great importance to consider the mobile device as a ubiquitous interface between state-of-the-art culture, everyday life and learning-outcome-oriented and student-centred learning in the classroom [17].

Ubiquitous learning means that students can learn *wherever* and *whenever* they want, but does not explicitly imply or emphasise the idea of establishing a fluid and smooth transition of learning experiences between different settings (e.g. classroom and informal learning). Seamless learning, on the other hand, seeks to create coherent and interdependent learning designs by considering learning in class and learning in context as one interconnected learning space without local and conceptual borders. The learning space is open [17] and rejects the dichotomy of formal/informal learning as two separate learning environments.

Seamlessness in informal learning environments also takes note of the context and changes thereof. In order to facilitate that learning in a situated, ambient, and open space-time can happen, the design ideally provides more than just content items [7].

To promote the approach of seamless learning, various studies suggest that 'seamlessness [is] achieved by bringing the same artefacts (data on mobile devices) into different social settings and times.' [8]. The learner, therefore, gathers, processes, and (re-)shares various artefacts (i.e. learning objects) in different social and local settings and considers the reflection on those artefacts as a holistic learning performance (independent from space, time and setting). In our approach, however, we aim to de-emphasise the content objects/artefacts, and instead focus on the learning interaction design for immersion, thereby creating a learner-centred overarching experience that is both, situated and outcome-oriented.

3   Pedagogic Design for Seamless Language Learning

Designing new seamless learning spaces is a key challenge for educators and language teachers. One of the issues connected to this is the lack of control of devices, content, and contexts, which takes the cognitive and technological support out of their hands. This often leads to criticism of the approach in the teaching community – sometimes even concluding in a general ban of new technologies such as smartphones in classrooms. Specht [20] calls it 'a top-challenge for most educators to adapt their instructional model for opening up and bridging to informal learning outside the classroom'. Keeping the attention and focus of learners on a set task is yet another difficulty rooted in the pedagogic design.

While we recognise these challenges, we would like to propose that modern technologies and informal learning opportunities, nevertheless, offer hitherto unknown possibilities of extending the learning experiences to authentic contexts from real life, which is especially useful for immersive FL learning. The unpredictability of real life situations reflects the challenges posed to language learners and leads them to seek out ways to cope with them linguistically and intellectually. Hence, this constitutes a key component of immersive language learning and would need to be addressed in the pedagogic design of building up competences in this area.

Following from this, we believe it to be of great importance that teachers recognise the opportunities available through seamless learning, and open their approaches to immersive pedagogic designs. Such designs do not focus on the teacher being in control of the learner's experience (context, environment, content, timeframe, etc.). Instead, the teacher's role becomes supportive and directive, focused on the orchestration of learning and learners. One key task is to bring diverse learner experiences together for shared social learning and to synchronise the class.

To support seamless learning designs one could follow the AICHE model [20, 21]. It builds on ambient information channels that form a frame for ubiquitous learning and synchronising real-world environments. It offers a way to connect and synchronise channels, artefacts, and users in a seamless learning environment and metacognitive learning processes. Synchronisation is at the core of every contextualised learning support. Synchronised channels can be mapped against relevant reference information in the instructional design which allows most artefacts and real-world objects with which we learn to be framed in the instructional context [21]. One example of this would be the social extensions of many mobile apps and e-portfolios that allow sharing, reflection and feedback within a social learning network.

4 Good Practice of Seamless Language Learning

4.1 Seamless Language Learning with Smartphones and e-Portfolios. An Overview

At the University of Teacher Education Vienna, the approach of seamless language learning is put into practice. Various curricular stakeholders and researchers suggest that lifelong learners at tertiary level should try to overcome pre-conceptualised learning borders. This is to say that a learner should not think in terms of formal vs. informal learning [15, 22]. Therefore, the approach of interdependent, interconnected, coherent and fluid education scenarios is of great relevance especially when educating future (language) teachers. In the context of language acquisition strategies and seamless learning, the dynamic approach of lifelong learning (LLL) should be noted. When addressing autonomous, fluid and self-regulated (language) learning scenarios within a tertiary context, e-portfolios come into play [23, 24]. Taking the curricular demands of the University of Teacher Education Vienna into consideration (especially EFL modules for pre-service English teachers), 'strategy model B e-portfolios' (i.e. reflection portfolios as a teaching/learning method [23]) are implemented in the pedagogical framework of various EFL seminars. The strategy model B e-portfolio can be characterised as follows:

- e-portfolios as teaching/learning method in individual courses (general description)
- reflection/learning process portfolio (portfolio type)
- high learning motivation through inspiring learner-centred arrangements. Training of key qualifications and increase of personal competency (main benefit for students)

- analysis, application, transfer of newly learned skills; promotion of overall competencies; quality control and development in teaching (curricular/institutional goals) [23]

Several chosen groups of EFL students use their smartphones (cf. opening up instructional models, considering real life learning situations by using technologies that meet the learners' zeitgeist in an informal and formal context) and the e-portfolio platform Mahara to bridge institution-based and informal learning contexts. Students are asked to use smartphones to create episodes of situated student-centred learning, which means that the curricular input of the EFL-lectures/seminars are extended with mobile-phone-assisted learning activities. The self-determined learning spaces (= episodes of situated learning) extend the 'learning path' of the student [25]. The following short didactic scenario exemplifies the seamless language learning approach further:

Curricular Input within a Classroom Based Context. During the EFL seminar, students receive theoretical and practical instruction on how to improve their monologic speaking skills (e.g. fluently talking about a certain topic [26–28]).

Creation of Linguistic Artefacts in Transferred Settings. In dedicated sessions (e.g. school practical studies for EFL students, etc.) students learn to use smartphone apps to create audio recordings (focusing on theoretical and practical aspects, how to focus on intonation, rhythm, stress, etc.). Then they are asked to produce several artefacts which supports the self-evaluation of their linguistic production (speaking skills): they record themselves in different situations (at university, at home, etc.) talking about certain seminar-related topics (e.g. the life of an English teacher in Vienna, documenting ELT-related activities, reflecting their lesson performances, and so forth) and articulating their ideas in the L2 independent of time and space. Alternatively, they can use an Avatar recording app like Voki (www.voki.com).

Sharing/Documenting/Discussing Artefacts in an e-Portfolio. After having recorded themselves and practised the act of monologic speaking about a certain topic (remedial drill-and-practice patterns), students are asked to upload the audio file (produced with their smartphone application) to their personal e-portfolio (in Mahara). The students then invite their peers and tutors to give constructive feedback on their spoken performance (feedback on discursive strategies, lexical/grammatical accuracy, coherent logic, etc.) [24].

4.2 Empirical and Didactical Evaluation of e-Portfolios and Seamless Language Learning

In order to back up the descriptive lines of argumentation concerning the use of e-portfolios and integrated seamless language learning, some empirical data [29, 30] will be presented. In the course of a research project at the University of Teacher Education Vienna (2011-2013, "The use of e-portfolios in teacher education"; with an emphasis on self-regulated language learning), the following scientific focal points were formulated:

1. What is the general perception (positive or negative) of Mahara among pre-service teachers after 1.5 years of e-portfolio usage in the course of school practical studies/EFL seminars?
2. Which Mahara-internal and external tools are being used in a certain didactical context (including reflection, feedback sessions, learning outcomes). How often are they used?

In the second year of the research project, a questionnaire with 27 questions (multiple choice and open questions) was designed for 220 students (pilot group, lower secondary and primary school pre-service teachers). 147 questionnaires were returned (i.e. 66,8 %). Furthermore, four semi-structured interviews were carried out with students.

Since it is part of the institution's curriculum to continuously use e-portfolios for pre-service teacher training especially in school practical studies, it seemed to be legitimate to ask for a general tendency concerning the perception of e-portfolios among students. The authors of the questionnaire deliberately formulated the following question in quite a general way in order to receive a quick response concerning perceptive tendencies: "If you had the chance to decide whether to continue using Mahara or not, how would you decide? O yes O no".

From the 147 respondents 85 (i.e. 57 %) want to continue using Mahara. From the perspective of the stakeholder and the project group, this figure is quite satisfactory, since speaking from a globally-semantic point of view a general majority of the students appreciate the use of Mahara, which can be seen as a solid basis for a continued use of e-portfolios with the determined need to constantly increase these figures in the implementation phase.

Analysing the data within the empirical segment "The use of Mahara-internal and external tools" (cf. research question 2, e.g. upload of audio files, etc., see above Sect. 4.1), the following recurring pattern concerning seamless learning outcomes can be recognised (mainly based on open questions): In certain groups (e.g. 3rd semester lower secondary school teachers and 1st semester primary school teachers) it can be seen that Mahara does not only serve as a simple archive of artefacts but also as a dynamic, seamless interface for communicative and self-regulated learning [31]; cf. students' recordings of spoken artefacts including reflective performance as a part of their tasks in the EFL seminars). Within this group, 23 people indicated that Mahara's journal (internal blog tool) is frequently used for reflective processes (blogging about their personal speaking performance). 27 students indicated that several external tools (e.g. audio player plug-ins) are continuously used to display or disseminate their produced artefacts (cf. audio recordings). Within the context of the semi-structured interviews with students, many of them explicitly uttered that the use of Mahara's journal function (blogging about your spoken performance, receiving constructive feedback on their linguistic performance by peers not only professors) in combination with simple but effective audio plug-ins (e.g. embed the recorded audio file into their personal learning environment) helped them to continuously become aware of their linguistic strengths and weaknesses (pronunciation, grammar, lexical mistakes) due to constructive chunks of feedback. Especially 'inhibited' (character attribute based on self-assessment by students in the course of semi-structured interviews) students had the chance to record their spoken performances over and over again until they believed their produced artefacts were suitable for meeting the demands of the original task (also considering in-between feedback by students and professors via the journal). Furthermore, they did not experience such a pressure as it would occur when performing their oral presentation within a formal classroom setting. Therefore, positive developments concerning certain learning outcomes (here: improvement of spoken performance) can be empirically noted. In addition, students reported that due to the fact various performative artefacts can be uploaded/edited/adapted (here: audio recordings) within an explicitly ubiquitous, dynamic and informal context (artefacts can be uploaded from almost everywhere), students can focus on their tasks/performance in familiar surroundings (e.g. at home) which often contributes to a more effective seamless learning experience.

Here, the e-portfolio does not only serve the purpose of a pure introspective self-reflection tool [32], but requires solid peer-to-peer learning (student-student, teacher-student) with a strong emphasis on seamless learning performances. The following four aspects of self- and peer-reflective learning can be noted:

- Product: Artefacts (e.g. blog posts about the student's spoken performance) can be reflected upon by their creators whether they do their job for which they were chosen. [Feedback/reflection on linguistic performance are mainly coherently uttered in a formal and informal context as one aspect of seamlessness]
- Process: The creators of e-portfolios can describe and reflect upon their methods used (e.g. new skills) and how they required them [e.g. learning diary, development of speaking skills]
- Person: The creators can document their trials or experiences that enabled them to grow and feel satisfaction or motivated them during the learning process [= seamless and immersive documentation of learning strategies in an authentic, mostly informal context]
- Problems: The learners should document their attempts to solve problems (including problem finding and problem solving) [e.g. peer feedback/error correction by students and teachers]

These aspects can possibly add 'visual evidence and historicity': [32] 'Storing and reflecting artefacts allows students to compare their efforts of several [weeks] ago with a present piece of work, so that it is possible to trace growth and development within a certain period'. [32].

Thus, e-portfolios in combination with smartphones 'will become a solid basis for social collaboration' [32] that help language learners to construct, improve, adapt and peer-review their linguistic competences within a curricular context that bridges informal and formal learning scenarios.

4.3   Benefits of Seamless Language Learning

By making students aware that the language learning designs can be considered as something fluid (formal and informal learning being coherently linked), unrestricted in space and time (ubiquitous production/reflection of learning products) and multi-sensory (using audio, video, images, etc.), they realise that learning need not be categorised either as strictly institutional or informal. The well-designed blend of lessons, mobile technology, and artefact curation tools like e-portfolios support the language learning process to appear more holistic without the constraints of traditional lesson structures. This fluid and ubiquitous learning process using different levels of interactivity and construction of knowledge/competences helps students become more aware of the fact that they can provide peer support or practise certain linguistic patterns (here the production of grammatically, lexically and topically coherent monologic spoken texts) whenever it suits them best.

Due to the technological simplicity of several audio recording or Avatar applications [33], students are able to record and re-record themselves as often as they like (whenever and wherever) and submit their final learning product when they think it meets the curricular demands. If the students are not really satisfied with their recording, they can bring it to the physical classroom or the virtual sharing space, discuss it with peers and teachers, adapt it, improve and finalise it. Here, seamless learning means establishing a fluent local interdependence of learning outcomes. Furthermore, students are given the chance to continuously reflect on and document progress by using an e-portfolio (cf. above).

Another benefit is the inherent flexibility of the learning activities. Whenever the students have another idea on how to improve their recordings, they can immediately access it via their smartphones or e-portfolios (from home, on the move, in class) and adapt it to the needs of the momentum. Therefore, seamless learning supports the idea of immediacy as a continuous, rapid reflection process. With the support of the tutor, their peers and the use of complementary technologies, students can overcome being mere recipients of transferred knowledge, but directors of their own learning.

The seamless scenario described above can be considered as "open" or "flexible", where formal and informal learning converges (since the learners can improve or modify their audio recordings anytime anywhere). Even more importantly, in this spatial and temporal openness, the formal learning design is extended into the "real world", and, therefore, includes specific cultural codes of discursive and behavioural patterns adapted to general frameworks of society, e.g. how to give constructive feedback on their peers' audio recordings, how to critically reflect on one's own linguistic performance, etc. What is more, the learning design becomes situated as learners are challenged with developing awareness of real-life contexts (i.e. situations they encounter while developing their artefacts). Due to the fact that the learners also continuously work or reflect on their learning products (their audio production) within an *everyday life* context, the learning experience per se becomes more authentic than the one in a traditional classroom-based situation.

5   Towards Digital Immersion and Seamlessness

We'd like to come back to the original concept of enabling digital language immersion using seamless learning designs. In our short example above (i.e. a seamless learning scenario), we captured one individual element of FL learning. To achieve digital immersion using the full potential of modern learning technologies, many targeted and complementary learning designs, addressing different linguistic and cultural competences such as comprehension, production or feedback/reflection skills need to be applied. These can be structured against expected outcomes along the lines of the Common European Framework of Reference for Languages (CEFR; [27]). Several attempts using augmented reality have already been undertaken and evaluated, including the description of requirements for a contextualised multi-platform learning framework [34].

This would in our opinion lead to the need of designing new learning spaces away from, but incorporating the classroom activities (blended designs). It requires the learning designer to think about new interfaces and the openness of the course, but, even more importantly, the expected outcomes. Learning in self-directed seamless spaces, naturally, becomes entirely outcome-oriented, due to the self-determination of the learner in organising and taking control of their own learning. While this sounds challenging in the beginning, the longer-term benefits are competent, confident lifelong learners.

What we would like to stress, however, is that immersion teaching has a firm rooting in cultural authenticity and this is often not served by language learning lessons, no matter how advanced the technology that is being used might be. Seamless scenarios developing cultural competences, therefore, should in our view become an integral part of seamless TELL. Understanding cultural concepts of a foreign language, regionalisms, dialects/accents and sociolects, therefore, need to be designed into the language learning experience and exposure of students. Designing cultural and contextual experiences for language learners can, in our opinion, lead to more comprehensive competence building, and the use of modern mobile, immersive and ambient technologies can provide the necessary connective environment to facilitate this.

References

1. NCR: National Center for Research on Cultural Diversity and Second Language Learning, Integrating Language and Content: Lessons from Immersion (1995). http://www.cal.org/resources/digest/ncrcds05.html)
2. Baker, C.: Foundations of Bilingual Education and Bilingualism. Multilingual Matters, Clevedon (1993)
3. Jones, C.: The Ulpan in Wales. A study in motivation. J. Multilingual Multicultural Dev. 12(3), 183–193 (1991)
4. Dalton-Puffer, C.: Outcomes and processes in Content and Language Integrated Learning (CLIL). Current research from Europe. Future Perspectives for English Language Teaching, N.N. (2008). http://www.univie.ac.at/Anglistik/Dalton/SEW07/CLIL%20research%20overview%20article.pdf
5. Lasagabaster, D., Sierra, J.-M.: Immersion and CLIL in English: more differences than similarities. ELT J. 64(4), 367–375 (2010). http://laslab.org/upload/immersion_and_clil_in_english:_more_differences_than_similarities.pdf
6. DeFreitas, S.: Learning in Immersive worlds - A review of game-based learning. E-Learning Series (2006). http://www.jisc.ac.uk/media/documents/programmes/elearninginnovation/gamingreport_v3.pdf

7. Börner, D., Kalz, M., Specht, M.: A conceptual framework for ambient learning displays. In: Joint Proceedings of the Work-in-Progress Poster and Invited Young Researcher Symposium for the 18th International Conference on Computers in Education, Putrajaya, Malaysia (2010). http://dspace.ou.nl/bitstream/1820/2827/1/ICCE_CUMTEL_submission. pdf
8. Gruber, M., Cooper, A., Voigt, C.: Seamless learning (U-Learn) (2012). http://www. learningfrontiers.eu/?q=content/seamless-learning-u-learn
9. Chan, T.-W., Roschelle, J., His, S., Sharples, M., Brown, T.: One-to-one technology-enhanced learning. An opportunity for global research collaboration. Res. Practice Tech. Enhanced Learn. **01**, 3–29 (2006)
10. Wong, L.-H., Looi, C.-K.: What seams do we remove in mobile assisted seamless learning? A critical review of the literature. Comput. Educ. **57**(4), 2364–2381 (2011)
11. Looi, C.-K., Seow, P., Zhang, B.H., So, H.-J., Chen, W., Wong, L.-H.: Leveraging mobile technology for sustainable seamless learning: a research agenda. Br. J. Educ. Technol. **41**(2), 154–169 (2010)
12. Cross, J.: Informal Learning. The other 80 % (2003). http://www.commonknowledge.org/ userimages/resources_peer_assist_guidelines+.pdf
13. Siemens, G.: Connectivism (2004). http://www.elearnspace.org/Articles/connectivism.htm
14. Cook, J., Pachler, N., Bachmair, B.: Ubiquitous mobility with mobile phones: a cultural ecology for mobile learning. E-Learn. Digit. Media **8**(3), 181–196 (2011)
15. Etxeberria, A.-L. (ed.): Global e-Learning. UDIMA, Open University, Madrid (2012)
16. Casey, J., Greller, W.: Jane Austen and the belly of the beast: commodification, technology and the open agenda in higher education. In: Presentation at the Goldsmiths Learning and Teaching Conference, London, UK, (30 May 2014). http://www.gold.ac.uk/gleu/confe rence2014
17. Wiley, D.: Openness, Dynamic Specialization, and the Disaggregated Future of Higher Education (2009). http://www.irrodl.org/index.php/irrodl/article/view/768/1415
18. Pachler, N., Bachmair, B., Cook, J.: Mobile learning. Structures, agency, practices. Springer Science + Business Media, New York (2010)
19. Strasser, T.T.: A change of paradigm with Web 2.0? Why Educational Apps might be worth a try. In: Etxeberria, A.-L. (ed.) Global e-Learning, pp. 135–144. UDIMA, Open University, Madrid (2012)
20. Specht, M.: connecting learning contexts with ambient information channels. In: Wong, L.H., Milrad, M., Specht, M. (eds.) Seamless Learning in the Age of Mobile Connectivity, pp. 121–140. Springer, Heidelberg (2015)
21. Specht, M.: Learning in a Technology-Enhanced World: Context in Ubiquitous Learning Support. Inaugural Address. Heerlen, The Netherlands: Open University of the Netherlands September 11 (2009). http://hdl.handle.net/1820/2034
22. European Commission: Digital Agenda for Europe. A Europe 2020 Initiative (2012). http:// eacea.ec.europa.eu/llp/about_llp/about_llp_en.php
23. Himpsl, K.: Implementation strategies for e-Portfolios in Austrian higher education. In: Baumgartner, P., Zauchner, S., Bauer, R. (eds.) The Potential of e-Portfolios in Higher Education, pp. 123–137. Studienverlag, Wien/Innsbruck/Bozen (2009)
24. Strasser, T., Knecht, H.: ePortfolios in school practical studies at Vienna University of Teacher Education – from theoretical considerations to practical implementation. In: Ravet, S. (ed.). EPIC ePortfolio and identity conference proceedings (2012). http://www.epforum. eu/proceedings/2012
25. Friedrich, K., Bachmair, B., Risch, M. (eds.): Mobiles Lernen mit dem Handy. Herausforderung und Chance für den Unterricht. Beltz, Weinheim (2011)

26. Byram, M. (ed.): The Common European framework of reference. The Globalisation of Language Education Policy. Multilingual Matters, Bristol (2012)
27. Council of Europe: Common European Framework of Reference for Languages. Learning, teaching, assessment. Language Policy Unit, Strasbourg (2001). http://www.coe.int/t/dg4/linguistic/Source/Framework_EN.pdf
28. Morrow, K.: Insights from the Common European Framework. Oxford University Press, Oxford (2004)
29. Strasser, T., Knecht, H.: e-Portfolios in den schulpraktischen Studien der PH Wien. In: Mayrberger, K., Waba, S., Schratz, M. (eds.) Journal für LehrerInnenbildung, Social Media in der Lehrerbildung, pp. 23-Facultas, Vienna (2013)
30. Empirical data based on questionnaires and semi-structured interviews, cf. www.mahara.phwien.ac.at and [28]
31. Baumgartner, P., Zauchner, S., Bauer, R. (eds.): The Potential of e-Portfolios in Higher Education. StudienVerlag, Innsbruck (2009)
32. Bauer, R.: Construction of one's identity. A student's view on the potential of e-Portfolios. In: Baumgartner, P., Zauchner, S., Bauer, R. (eds.) The Potential of e-Portfolios in Higher Education, pp. 173–183. Studienverlag, Wien/Innsbruck/Bozen (2009)
33. Strasser, T.: Quick 'n dirty. The use of internet tools in the EFL classroom. In: Scholes, J. (ed.) Revista: New Routes 51, pp. 14–18. DISAL, Brazil (2013)
34. De Jong, T.: Contextualised Mobile Media for Learning. Open University, Heerlen (2011)

How to Detect Programming Skills of Students?

Štefan Pero[(⊠)]

Institute of Computer Science, Pavol Jozef Šafárik University, Košice, Slovakia
stefan.pero@student.upjs.sk

Abstract. The teaching of introductory programming is still problem. In this work we focus on designing the technique to detect and recognize programming patterns from student's program source codes. First, we describe a source code in the form of an Abstract Syntax Tree (AST) and in its transformation to XML format. The detection of patterns is done with the SLEUTH algorithm for frequent subgraph mining on trees. We provide experiments using real data from a programming course at our university. In the paper, we discuss the relation between patterns. We also discuss how combinations and constructions of patterns can define some kind of skills and how we can categorize the skills into several skill levels according to their complexity. Finally, we propose some use cases and further directions of our research.

Keywords: Pattern · Source code · Student · Skill

1 Introduction

The teaching of introductory programming is still problem. Many models for teaching programming have been suggested and described in the literature. According to interviews with teachers they do not relate to such models.

One of the best-known problems in educational data mining (EDM) is predicting student's performance [8]. A great deal of algorithms have been applied to predict academic success of students. However, we are interested mainly in the following issues/questions: *What lies in the background and prerequisities of students' success? What skills do students have and what is their level?* As teachers we often seek ways to help our students. We try to analyse teir learning process and we try to lead them to better results.

We are inspired by a real situation from the programming course at our university. Students solve programming tasks and produce source codes what is a special in comparison of mathematical problem solving. According to the provided source codes teacher can more precisely evaluate students' solution. Evaluation of the solutions for the tasks solved by students is a complex process driven mainly by subjective evaluation criteria of a given teacher. Each teacher is somehow biased meaning how strict she is in assessing grades to solutions. Besides the teacher's bias there are also some other factors contributing to grading, for example, teachers can make mistakes, the grading scale is too rough-grained or too fine grained, etc. Latent programming skills of students are somehow "encoded"

© Springer International Publishing Switzerland 2015
M. Ebner et al. (Eds): EiED 2014, CCIS 486, pp. 63–72, 2015.
DOI: 10.1007/978-3-319-22017-8_6

in their source codes provided. Automatic detection of these latent skills (with or without the assistance of the teacher) remains still an open issue.

The objective of our research is to design a new, extended version of educational recommendation where the role of the teacher related to the student and his tasks in the educational process is strong and should be integrated to the recommendation process in contrast to traditional techniques which consider more or less only the entities of the student and the task. We call such an extended technique as supervised educational recommender system the general model of which is presented in [10]. For instance students provides their feedback to the tasks and tasks are recommended to students. The main goal is to improve programming skills of students provided by recommendation of those tasks evaluated by the theacher to the student which more likely improve her skills.

Pardos and Heffernan presented a model called "Knowledge tracing" [7] and they used it to model students' knowledge and learning over the time assuming that all students share the same initial prior knowledge. To allow per student prior information to be incorporated, they introduced an elegant way within a Bayesian networks framework that fits for individualized as well as skill specific parameters [6]. However, by considering the needed (listed) skills as attributes of the task, it is straightforward to use them also as features in prediction models [9]. Desmarais, Naceur and Beheshti [3] introduce different linear models of student skills for small, static student test data that does not contain missing values. They compare the predictive performance of their model to the traditional psychometric Item Response Theory approach, and the k-nearest-neighbors approach. In [1] they present wrapper-based method for finding the number of latent skills.

This work focuses on designing the technique to detect and recognize programming patterns from students' source program codes. Using real data, we illustrate how do patterns related to skills of students predefined by the teacher (author of the task) are discovered. The contributions of this work are the following:

- We introduce a model for representing source codes in a tree-structure.
- We propose a simple approach to detect patterns in source codes utilizing pattern mining algorithm. We illustrate the complete process of pattern detection on a real-world dataset provided us by our colleagues at our university.

2 The Proposed Approach

Our approach is based on the pattern detection from source codes and on the analysis of the relationships between the found patterns and the skills for programming tasks pre-defined by the teacher. We present our strategy to detect patterns in source codes.

2.1 Source Code Representation

Representation of source codes is a critical issue in designing the process of pattern recognition. We utilize a representation scheme of source codes in the form of Abstract Syntax Trees (AST), an example of which is illustrated in the Fig. 1. AST provide detailed information about the source code which can be used for various types of analysis [4]. Various information about a source code, especially syntactic information, is represented in the form of a tree in which nodes represent entities of a source code and edges represent relations between these entities, both having their own annotations that denote also some semantic properties.

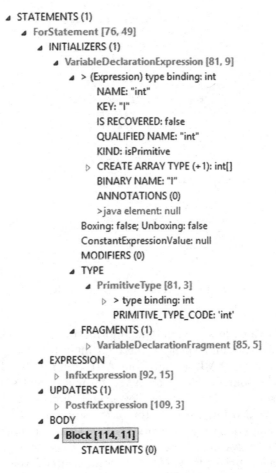

Fig. 1. AST structure for a *for loop* in Java.

AST use a tree-like structure to represent the source code in a top-down manner. For example, Java applications are represented at the top level as applications, classes and packages while at lowest levels as methods, functions, declarations, expressions, and identifiers. Internal nodes of the AST structure represent non-terminal phrases such as statements, operations, functions and the leaf nodes represent terminal symbols, such as identifiers, and empty declarators. Edges denote tree attributes represented as mappings between AST nodes. AST nodes correspond to programming language constructs such as If-Statements, For-Statements, While-Statements. For more details on AST we refer to [5].

```
<ForStatement>
    <Initializers>
        <VariableDeclarationExpression>
            <PrimitiveType>int</PrimitiveType>
            <VariableDeclarationFragmen>i
            </VariableDeclarationFragment>
        </VariableDeclarationExpression>
    <Initializers>
    <Expression>
    <InfixExpression>
        <LeftOperand>i</LeftOperand>
        <Operator>'<'</Operator>
        <RightOperand>10</RightOperand>
    </InfixExpression>
    </Expression>
    <Updaters>
    <PostfixExpression>
        <Operand>i</Operand>
        <Operator>'++'</Operator>
    </PostfixExpression>
    </Updaters>
    <Body><Body/>
</ForStatement>
```

Fig. 2. AST in XML format on the level 1.

Since AST contains lots of abundant information from a pattern detection point of view, we have implemented our own filter to generate a representation of a source code in XML format from AST (see the Fig. 2). The resulting representation of a source code in an XML format provides us with a better abstraction of a source code in different levels and allows us to better specify its important parts needed for the next step of our approach. For example, at the lowest level of abstraction only elements without their attributes are taken into account. With the increasing level of abstraction we consider more attributes of the elements a the source code. We have identified three levels of abstraction of source code representation which are introduced in the Table 1).

2.2 Pattern Mining

In our approach we use SLEUTH, an efficient algorithm for mining frequent, unordered, embedded subtrees in a database of labeled trees [12]. Mining frequent trees is very useful for mining semi-structured data in different domains. Several

Table 1. Identified levels of abstraction.

Level	Elements	Attributes
1	All	None
2	All	All
3	Selected	Selected

other tree mining algorithms have been proposed including TreeMiner, Free-TreeMiner, FreqT, TreeFinder, CMTreeMiner, they mine embedded/induced, ordered/unordered trees (for more details, see [13]).

Given the particular source codes, first, we represent them in relevant trees in XML format at the given level of abstraction. Consider a representation illustrated in the Fig. 3, which shows an example tree of a source code represented in an XML format at the second level of abstraction where each vertex contains some additional attributes (XML element and its attributes). Second, we apply SLEUTH on the prepared dataset of trees with the lowest level of abstraction. The aim is to find all patterns (frequent, unordered, embedded subtrees) in the input dataset. An example of such a pattern is shown in the Fig. 3.

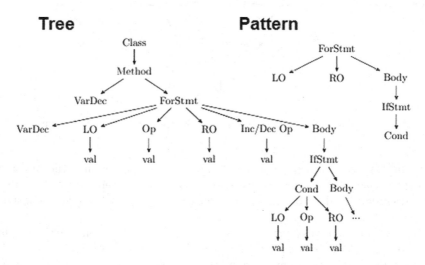

Fig. 3. Example of a tree and a pattern, where *LO = LeftOperand, RO = Right-Operand, Op = Operator, VarDec = VariableDeclaration, val = value.*

We are especially interested in so-called *maximal frequent patterns*, i.e. maximal frequent subtrees which are defined as those frequent subtrees none of which proper supertrees are frequent [2].

Finally, we cluster the resulting maximal frequent patterns (since many of them may be similar) and extract a set of representative patterns from each cluster of maximal frequent patterns.

2.3   Relation Between Patterns and Skills

Consider the following instance of the *for loop* construction in the Java programming language.

$$\text{for(int i=0;i<5;i++)\{...\}} \tag{1}$$

To understand this construction of a for loop, and thus, to be able to use it during programming, we must first understand the following four programming concepts we call *prerequisites* for the for loop the model of which are illustrated in the Fig. 4:

- variable declaration (`int i`)
- variable assigment (`i=0`)
- relational operators (`i<5`)
- increment/decrement operators (`i++`)

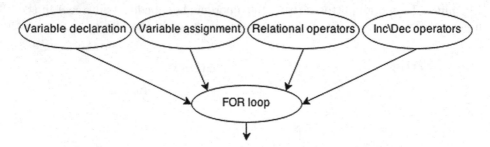

Fig. 4. The model of the prerequisites of the *for loop* construction.

An important issue to mention here is "The whole is greater than the sum of its parts" principle. For example, if one knows all of these prerequisites for the for loop individually it does not necessarily mean that she is also able to construct a for loop itself.

Since all prerequisites as well as their combinations and constructions define some kind of *skills* we can categorize the skills into several *skill levels* according to their complexity. We identified four skill levels which are introduced in the Table 2.

The complex constructions composed from skills at lower levels can described *patterns?*

Finally, each representative pattern consists of skills. It is very important to correctly recognize and difficult to correctly describe for teachers and educators.

Table 2. Skills levels.

Skill level	Examples of skills
1	variables, arrays, operators, ...
2	loops, conditions, recursion, ...
3	functions, inheritance, polymorphism, abstract classes, recursion,...
4	complex constructions, programs, ...

3   First Experiments

Experiments were performed with a real-world dataset, labeled "PAC"[1]. The dataset contains the following information about students' solutions: *studentID, taskID, teacherID, grade, review, solution (source code)*. For our experiments, however, we used only the following tuples:

$$(studentID, taskID, grade, solution). \qquad (2)$$

Main characteristics of the dataset are described in the Table 3. Each task belong to one set of tasks, i.e. we consider a set of tasks as one complex task containing several subtasks.

Table 3. Characteristics of the dataset used

Dataset PAC	#Students	#Sets	#Tasks	#Codes
2011/2012 A	82	7	33	578
2011/2012 B	36	9	21	381
2012/2013 A	85	6	28	769
2012/2013 B	33	10	20	397
2013/2014 A	78	7	31	510

We realized experiments on the sets of tasks according to the described steps of our approach above, such as representation in AST, conversion to XML, pattern mining with SLEUTH and clustering the maximal patterns. When converting AST to our above defined XML format, we used the lowest level of abstraction.

The result shown in Fig. 5 refer to the number of patterns and the number of maximal patterns detected in the data for different sets of tasks. Using maximal patterns we are able to filter out repetitive and meaningless patterns. In pattern mining method we used support $0.8, 0.9, 1$ corresponding to 80%, 90% and 100% coverage, respectively.

---

[1] Collected from the "Programming Algorithms Complexity" course at the Institute of Computer Science at Pavol Jozef Šafárik University during the years 2011–2014. The course consists of two parts: (A) Introduction to programming and OOP, (B) Introduction to algorithms and computations.

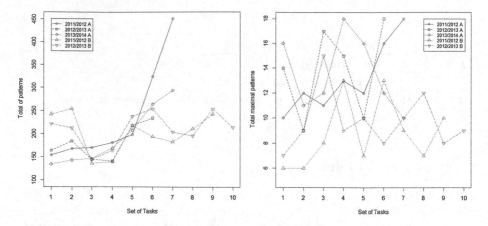

Fig. 5. The number of detected patterns and maximal patterns with support=1 (i.e. 100 % coverage)

4   Use Cases and Future Work

Recommendation. In [10] we proposed a framework for an educational recommender system enriched by the role of the teacher. We call it Supervised Recommender System (SRS) which consists of three important components, the *student*, the *task* and the *teacher*, generally representing a *user*, a *item* and a *supervisor*, respectively. The idea behind SRS is that the student provides a solution (source code) according to her programming skills. The teacher verifies the fulfillment of his requirements on the solution and provides a feedback on the student, i.e. a grading and/or a textual comment. An interpretation of such feedback could be *how student's skills meet teacher's requirements*. Using this feedback and analyzing the provided source code we could derive student's skills (patterns) and recommend those tasks to her which can more likely improve her skills. Here we have to mention, that teachers' evaluations might contain inconsistencies as we showed in our previous work [11].

Classification. By analyzing of source codes we can classify students' solutions to different classes and find frequent programming patterns discriminating right solutions from the wrong ones. Consecutively, we can use these patterns to classify unevaluated solutions to different classes. In our first experiments we used the representation of source codes at the lowest level of abstraction and frequent patterns were mined from all the solutions (source codes) not taking into account the quality/correctness of these solutions. In further work we will focus on mining patterns discriminating correct solutions from the wrong ones for what we intend to use more detailed representations of source codes at the second and third levels.

Plagiarism detection. Patterns detection might be also used for detection of plagiarism among students. The aim is to detect and point out similarities between source-code files. Naturally, these similarities should be carefully investigated by the academic to taking actions for plagiarism against the students, but the right detection of plagiarism is the first step to provide better check of codes by academic and can be used as evidence in the event that the academic decides to take matters further.

Didactics. Programming patterns and the detected skills might be very helpful for teachers to gain better insight to the programming habits of students, their main weaknesses and strengths. Patterns can uncover some common mistakes students make during programming, and thus, help to improve the didactic techniques for programming. It would be also interesting to analyze how the detected patterns in different skills levels (see the Table 2) differ from each other. For this reason we have recently started a collaboration with our colleagues working in the field of didactics of informatics which will further analyze the patterns resulting from our model.

5   Conclusions

We presented a model for mining patterns in source codes in order to map these patterns to corresponding programming skills. The proposed model consists of several phases such as source code representation in the form of AST and its transformation to XML at different levels, mining frequent maximal patterns and choose their representatives by utilizing clustering techniques. Since our work is in its beginning we provided only some early-bird experiments. We have also discussed four use cases of the mined programming patterns we would like to focus on in our future work.

Acknowledgments. This publication is the result of the Project implementation: **University Science Park TECHNICOM for Innovation Applications Supported by Knowledge Technology**, ITMS: 26220220182, supported by the Research & Development Operational Programme funded by the ERDF and was partially supported by the research grants *VEGA 1/0475/14* and *VVGS-PF-2013-102*.

References

1. Beheshti, B., Desmarais, M.C., Naceur, R.: Methods to find the number of latent skills. International Educational Data Mining Society (2012)
2. Chi, Y., Muntz, R., Nijssen, S., Kok, J.: Frequent subtree mining - an overview (2005)
3. Desmarais, M.C., Naceur, R., Beheshti, B.: Linear models of student skills for static data. In: UMAP Workshops (2012)
4. Maruyama, K., Yamamoto, S.: A case tool platform using an xml representation of java source code. In: Proccedings of Fourth IEEE International Workshop on Source Code Analysis and Manipulation (2004)
5. Mamas, E., Kontogiannis, K.: Towards portable source code representations using xml. In: Proceedings of the Seventh Working Conference on Reverse Engineering (2000)

6. Pardos, Z.A., Gowda, S.M., Baker, R.S.J.D., Heffernan, N.T.: The sum is greater than the parts: ensembling models of student knowledge in educational software. In: Proceedings of ACM's Knowledge Discovery and Datamining (KDD) Explorations (2012)
7. Pardos, Z.A., Heffernan, N.T.: Modeling Individualization in a bayesian networks implementation of knowledge tracing. In: De Bra, P., Kobsa, A., Chin, D. (eds.) UMAP 2010. LNCS, vol. 6075, pp. 255–266. Springer, Heidelberg (2010)
8. Romero, C., Ventura, S.: Data mining in education. Wiley Interdisciplinary Reviews: Data Mining and Knowledge Discovery (2012)
9. Thai-Nghe, N., Drumond, L., Horváth, T., Schmidt-Thieme, L.: Multi-relational factorization models for predicting student performance. In: ACM SIGKDD 2011 Workshop on Knowledge Discovery in Educational Data (2009)
10. Pero, Š.: Modeling programming skills of students in an educational recommender system. In: Carberry, S., Weibelzahl, S., Micarelli, A., Semeraro, G. (eds.) UMAP 2013. LNCS, vol. 7899, pp. 401–404. Springer, Heidelberg (2013)
11. Pero, Š., Horváth, T.: Detection of inconsistencies in student evaluations. In: Proceedings of the 5th International Conference on Computer Supported Education (2013)
12. Zaki, M.J.: Efficiently mining frequent embedded unordered trees. Fundamenta Informaticae (2005)
13. Zaki, M.J.: Efficiently mining frequent trees in a forest Algorithms and applications. IEEE Trans. Knowl. Data Eng. **17**(8), 1021–1035 (2005)

Binding Daily Physical Environments to Learning Activities with Mobile and Sensor Technology

Bernardo Tabuenca[✉], Marco Kalz, and Marcus Specht

Welten Institute, Research Centre for Learning, Teaching and Technology,
Open University of the Netherlands, Heerlen, The Netherlands
{bernardo.tabuenca,marco.kalz,marcus.specht}@ou.nl

Abstract. Lifelong learners' activities are scattered along the day, in different locations and making use of multiple devices. Most of the times they have to merge learning, work and everyday life making difficult to have an account on how much time is devoted to learning activities and learning goals. Indeed, learning experiences are disrupted and there is a lack of solutions to integrate daily life activities and learning in the same process. On the other hand, smartphones are becoming a universal learning device facilitating new tools and ways of interaction that can be smoothly embedded into daily life. This manuscript presents the NFC LearnTracker, a mobile tool proposing the user to introspect his autobiography as a learner to identify successful physical learning environments, mark them with sensor tags, bind them to self-defined learning goals, keep track of the time invested on each goal with a natural interface, and monitor the learning analytics. This work implies a suitable tool for lifelong learners to bind scattered activities keeping them in a continuing learning flow. The NFC LearnTracker is released under open access licence with the aim to foster adaptation to further communities as well as to facilitate the extension to the increasing number of sensor and NFC tags existent in the market.

Keywords: Lifelong learning · Self-regulation · Natural interaction · NFC · Personal learning ecologies

1 Introduction

Self-organized learning is one of the critical competences for individuals to cope with societal challenges and resulting changing demands on job markets. A survey by the European Commission has identified time, location and conflicts with other activities as the core barriers to lifelong learning [1]. Nowadays, lifelong learners are confronted with a broad range of activities they have to manage everyday. In most cases they have to combine learning activities, professional and private life linking formal and non-formal learning activities. In the setting of an adult lifelong learner this is especially difficult as in most cases, interests might be highly distributed over different domains and keeping up learning needs an extra effort. One of the main challenges here is the bridging of learning activities between different contexts.

© Springer International Publishing Switzerland 2015
M. Ebner et al. (Eds): EiED 2014, CCIS 486, pp. 73–84, 2015.
DOI: 10.1007/978-3-319-22017-8_7

Mobile seamless learning technology can offer solutions to address this problem. Seamless learning was first defined as a learning style where a learner can learn in a variety of scenarios and in which they can switch from one scenario or context to another easily and quickly, with the personal device as a mediator [2]. Succeeding, Wong et al. [3] identified ten gaps in seamless learning support: (1) Encompassing formal and informal learning; (2) Encompassing personalized and social learning; (3) Across time; (4) Across locations; (5) Ubiquitous knowledge access; (6) Encompassing physical and digital worlds; (7) Combined use of multiple device types; (8) Seamless switching between multiple learning tasks; (9) Knowledge synthesis; (10) Encompassing multiple pedagogical or learning activity models. Lately, a learner-centric view of mobile seamless learning [4] suggests that *a seamless learner should be able to explore, identify and seize boundless latent opportunities that his daily living spaces may offer to him (mediated by technology), rather than always being inhibited by externally-defined learning goals and resources.* For lifelong learners several key aspects have to be highlighted that are essential problems:

- No support for learning activities across locations, devices, and environments. There is very little research on how to link the different everyday contexts of lifelong learners and their learning activities in these different settings. (Seam 3, 4)
- Linking learning activities with everyday life activities and the physical world objects. Everyday life events trigger different activities that lead to learning events. The linking between the self-directed learning of lifelong learners and their everyday environment is not foreseen in todays learning technology (Seam 1, 2, 7, 8)
- Supporting reflection on learning activities and personal project in heterogeneous environments making use of different technologies (Seam 6, 9, 10).

In summary there is little support for lifelong learners that typically try to learn in different contexts, are busy with multiple parallel learning tracks, and must align or relate their learning activities to everyday leisure and working activities. Candy [5] has summarized four components of self-directed lifelong learning. These are self-*monitoring, self-awareness, self-management* (planning of learning) and last but not least *meta-learning*. To date, there is little technological support to enable learners in conducting these different activities across contexts and locations. A recent survey to lifelong learners on mobile usage habits reveals that there is an association between the type of learning activity being performed (read, write, listen, watch) and the specific daily space where it takes place [6]. Hence, there is a need to provide suitable tools for lifelong learners to facilitate bridging learning experiences in a seamless flow. In this paper Near Field Communication (NFC) is proposed as an instantiation for natural interaction with mobile devices and for seamless integration of technology in lifelong learning.

The following section reviews previous research of scientific work where NFC has been used with learning purposes. Section 2 identifies the four pillars sustaining the design of a mobile tool for self-regulated support. In Sect. 3 the core features are described and the results of a prototype formative evaluation are presented. Finally, conclusions are discussed and future work is described.

Using NFC Sensor Tags for Bridging Seams and Natural Interaction. *Natural User Interfaces* and the *Internet of Things* have been predicted to have an impact on education in the short term [7]. Tagged objects are widely accepted and the number of connected devices could reach 50 billion by 2020 [8]. Different tagging methods (e.g. visual codes, text recognition, image recognition) allow enriching physical objects of the world with educational resources [9]. Moreover, the prominent adoption of NFC readers in mobile devices has moved this technology from an innovator to an early adopter phase. This frictionless technology will enrich our environment facilitating natural interactions with daily physical objects. NFC simplifies and reduces several actions to a single action of narrow contact (zero click overhead). These small exchanges of information between devices that occur almost instantaneously have been recently coined as *micro-interactions* [10].

Recent work reviews scientific literature in which NFC technology has been used with learning purposes [11]. More specifically, [12] present some of the potentials NFC technology brings for teaching and learning materials in formal education: distributing learning/teaching materials in face-to-face classrooms; enriching printed materials; sharing materials among students; delivery of practical work; bind physical actions to social networks; access to control materials; identification of students in examinations. Likewise, there is an increasing number of empirical studies using NFC technology in field trip excursions [13, 14], connecting digital and physical worlds [15–17] or combining this technology within Learning Management Systems [18]. Nevertheless, NFC has not been used to tackle the problems of lifelong learners. In the following we will frame and integrate these approaches according to the model of Candy [5] introduced in Sect. 1.

The work from Ebner and Maierhuber highlight the incompatibility between existing NFC-tags and NFC-readers as one of the main barriers blocking further expansion of the NFC technology [12]. For example, chips produced by one specific manufacturer perfectly work with their own tags but, other tags are not readable by chips produced by other manufacturers although their data format is based on the standard. It is one of the goals of this research to implement a generic open source architecture to facilitate its extension across NFC readers and tags.

2 Design of the NFC LearnTracker

The NFC LearnTracker is a standalone application developed for NFC-enabled Android (4.03 or above) devices released in March 2014 in Google Play[1]. The NFC LearnTracker uses an embedded database for local storage in the same application software to avoid privacy issues of sharing data. The NFC LearnTracker is part of a larger research (Lifelong Learning Hub Project) aiming to give ubiquitous support for lifelong learners. It has been released trusting open source code license, made available

---

[1] NFC LearnTracker in Google Play. https://play.google.com/store/apps/details?id=org.ounl. lifelonglearninghub.

in a repository[2] to be downloaded, customized and further extended to different learning environments, LMSs, or communities. This section presents the NFC LearnTracker as mobile seamless tool for self-regulated learning that aims to cover the following gaps in lifelong learners' learning process:

1. No support for learning activities across locations, devices and environments.
2. No linking between learning activities and everyday life.
3. No feedback on lifelong learning activities.
4. Incompatibility between NFC-tags and NFC-readers.

2.1 Self-regulation Across Contexts with Mobile Learning Analytics

The NFC LearnTracker has been designed based on the seamless notion that lifelong learners can learn in a variety of scenarios switching from one scenario or context to another easily and quickly, using the personal device as a mediator. Figure 1 illustrates how daily life activities and learning activities are combined in a continuing process. The tool presented in this section has been conceptualized on the idea that mobile technology can be smoothly integrated in daily life activities whenever interacting with it requires the least number of clicks possible (zero) and the duration of any interaction with the tool lasts not longer than 20 s.

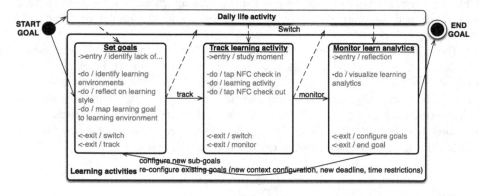

Fig. 1. UML state diagram: life cycle in lifelong learning goal's

Butler and Winne [19] describe the Self-Regulated Learning Model as an iterative process comprising four sequential stages: (1) interpretation of own learning paths and task queuing; (2) cognitive process of defining goals and monitoring the progress; (3) perform the learning activity; (4) interpretation of external feedback. Similar and focusing on lifelong learners, Candy [5] proposes a learner-centric model with four stages (See Sect. 1). Hereby we describe in a narrative way [20] how these stages have been covered with the NFC LearnTracker using the scenario of Miguel, a PhD student

---

[2] Lifelong Learning Hub's code repository. https://code.google.com/p/lifelong-learning-hub/.

aiming to combine daily life activity (family, work, leisure) with learning activities towards the accomplishment of his doctoral degree.

Set Goals. Miguel wants to improve his academic writing, develop his skills to make effective presentations in public, broaden his English vocabulary, and set aside time to read scientific literature. As he engages in these learning tasks, he draws on knowledge and beliefs constructing an interpretation of each task's properties and requirements [19]. In fact, Miguel frequently introspects his autobiography as a learner to identify which learning environment fits better to which learning task upon his learning style or time availability [21]. This stage covers the *"Planning for learning"* and *"self awareness"* stages in the self-regulation model for lifelong learners [5]. Analogously, Butler and Winne [19] situate the stage of *"setting goals"* within the cognitive system stressing its key importance in shaping the process of self-regulated learning.

In this stage (first box in Fig. 1), Miguel reflects on his learning style mapping learning goals to frequently used learning environments and tagging them with NFC tags (See examples in Fig. 3). Whenever Miguel configures his goals in the NFC LearnTracker, he takes a NFC tag, taps it with his NFC enabled mobile device so the interface in Fig. 2a is displayed. He characterizes the goal with a name, specifies the expected outcome when he accomplishes the goal, foresees how much time (in minutes) will he devote to this goal on daily basis, and finally indicates his expected date to finish the goal. Sticking a NFC tag on a physical learning object enables the connection of a variety of tracking data with the learning activity as Miguel can identify how much time does he use a specific device for reading (e.g. tablet, book, laptop), the location where he devotes more time to learn or the least productive days of the week. The learning goals dashboard (Fig. 2b) lists all the goals configured by the user.

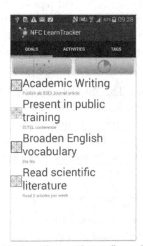

a). Linking a purple NFC tag to *Academic Writing* learning goal

b). Learning goals configured by the user

c). "Check-in" registered for *Academic Writing* and event history

Fig. 2. Binding goals to tagged learning environments via NFC LearnTracker

Perform Learning Activity. Miguel, as most of the lifelong learners [6], recurs to specific locations (e.g. desktop, coach) and moments (e.g. waiting times, transitions) to accomplish his learning activities. In addition, Miguel is interested to know how much time he devotes to his learning goals during the day and along the week. Hence, Miguel needs a tool with natural interaction, otherwise he will not bother to track short learning moments (e.g. fifteen minutes writing, Fig. 3a; twenty minutes reading, Fig. 3b; ten minutes listening podcasts, Fig. 3c; three minutes watching videos, Fig. 3d), and as result these moments will never be accounted as learning time. Hence, the NFC LearnTracker harvests all learning moments accounting them as real learning time with frictionless interactions. Both self-regulation models [5, 19] situate this stage out of the scope of the cognitive system.

| a). Write an article taking the first coffee in the morning at work | b). Reading scientific literature during waiting times | c). Listening English podcasts commuting to work, college, gym... | d). Watch top presenters' videos during commercial breaks |

Fig. 3. Learning activities (write, read, listen, watch) bound to daily learning environments

In this stage (second box in Fig. 1) Miguel taps the associated NFC-tag every time he wants to start *check-in* / stop *check-out* a learning activity. Figure 2c illustrates with a red dot the moment in which time devoted to the goal "*Academic Writing*" is being recorded as an effect of tapping the tag once. The history of the subsequent events is registered as a log.

Monitor Learning Activities. The NFC LearnTracker features learning analytics when defined as "*the measurement, collection, analysis and reporting of data about learners and their contexts, for purposes of understanding and optimising learning and the environments in which it occurs*" [22]. Monitoring the state in learning activity can motivate the user towards the accomplishment of a learning goal. By comparing evolving states of a task to goals creates conditional knowledge that is the basis for further action. This cognitive process has been defined as "*internal feedback*" [19], "*self monitoring*", and "*understanding how to learn*" [5] in the previously cited self-regulation models. The cues identified by the user in this process facilitate the recognition of his learning patterns and as a result, the constant update of his autobiography as a learner.

In this stage (see third box in Fig. 1), Miguel can monitor his learning analytics on a specific goal, or as overall performance. Siemens [23] stressed that the focus of learning analytics is exclusively on the learning process. Hence, the NFC LearnTracker tracks and visualizes data about the learning process within the specific personal learning context for which they were configured by the lifelong learner, and independently from the content (subject, topic, etc.) that is learned in the process. The NFC LearnTracker features a charting library[3] for Android applications facilitating the implementation of several visualizations. As of date December 2014, the NFC LearnTracker provides the following visualizations with the aim to foster understanding on learning habits, optimise learning, and, bind successful learning environments:

1. *Percentage of Time Invested on Each Learning Goal.* Learning activities are scattered along the day in different locations or transitions. This feature provides lifelong learners an overall summary on how much time is devoted to learning goals. Figure 4a illustrates how percentage of total time and number of minutes are presented in a pie chart. This visualization can be used by lifelong learners to compare time invested on his learning goals, identify priorities to accomplish goals, and, patterns regarding preferences for specific learning environments, devices or learning activities (read, watch, write, listen).

2. *Distribution of Learning Moments Along the Day.* Every lifelong learners performs differently in the sense that some of us prefer to do learning activities that require a higher cognitive load or concentration in early morning (scientific reading or writing), or do the ones that require least cognitive load (watch videos or dispatch emails) while sat on the couch at night during every commercial pause on TV. Lifelong learners are intrinsically interested to identify patterns in their learning experiences and scaffold their autobiography as a learner to better distribute learning activities in forthcoming goals. Figure 4b illustrates the distribution of the learning moments during the day (X axis 0..24) for a whole week (Y axis 1..7). Each spot (square, triangle, circle) identifies when the learning activity started.

3. *Monitoring Accomplished Goals.* Monitoring is of crucial importance in relation to the development as a self-regulated learner. Monitoring is the cognitive process that assesses states of progress to goals and generates feedback that can guide further action [19]. Figure 4c illustrates a representation of accomplished learning time versus expected time towards a learning goal NFC LearnTracker.

2.2 An Open Source Architecture Facilitating Extension Across NFC Readers and NFC Tags

There is a huge number of NFC tags available in the market. An NFC tag is a small passive (no battery) device that contains a microchip attached to a small loop antenna. When an NFC reader such as a mobile phone scans the tag, it powers up and wirelessly transfers information such as a web address, text or a command for an app. NFC tags are typically printed stickers, but they can be also enclosed in NFC products such as wristbands, hang tags and other artefacts.

---

[3] AChartEngine Library: https://code.google.com/p/achartengine/.

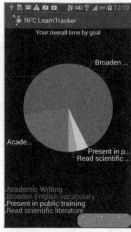

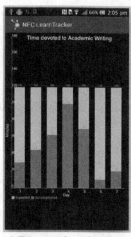

a) Quantity of time invested in learning goals (Percentage or overall time and number of minutes)

b) Distribution of learning moments along the day in the last 7 days

c) Foreseen learning time (orange) versus effective time invested (in purple) on *Academic Writing* in the week

Fig. 4. Learning analytics in NFC LearnTracker

There is no way to create an app capable to interpret the information encoded in every NFC tag available on the market. Nevertheless, it is possible to provide suitable guidance on how to extend the software to be compatible with further tags and readers. All NFC enabled phones currently on the market can read a web address (URI) or text. The NFC LearnTracker features NFC standards [24] (Fig. 5), namely, *UriRecord* tag is used to launch an URL in the mobile's browser, *TexRecord* tag is used to complete a text field within an app in the mobile, and *SmartPosters* tags is used in public static commercials to launch multimedia on user's device. Moreover, the LearnTracker has been developed following an architecture that facilitates its extension to more complex NFC tasks like command execution, and to enable the compatibility across NFC-tags and NFC-readers. When extending the use of tool to a new tag standart type, a new class must be created implementing the interface *IParseNdefRecord* so the methods *getId()* to indicate a unique identifier for the tag (e.g. http://www.ou.nl/293903843),

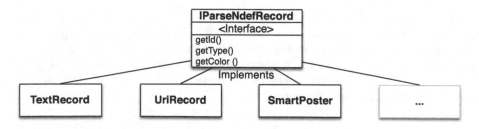

Fig. 5. Tag extension in NFC LearnTracker

getType() to indicate the name of the standard type (e.g. UriRecord), and *getColor()* to indicate the colour in RGB hex that will be used in the charts to identify the mapped goal (e.g. acdced).

3 Formative Evaluation

This tool was presented to 14 Ph.D. students attending to a workshop in March 2014. The concept of lifelong learning and the scope of the research were introduced and the problems described in the introduction section of the current manuscript were enumerated. With this focus in mind, the tool was presented for 30 min as a potential solution to those problems providing practical examples, making a demo with physical learning environments where the tool can be applied and highlighting the natural interaction of the NFC micro-interactions. After that, participants completed a questionnaire containing eight 5-likert-scale questions prompting the participants to reflect and rate the potential of the tool to: manage learning goals; foster awareness on preferred learning environments; integrate learning with daily life activities; learning activities across contexts; set aside time to learn on regular basis; adjust goals high enough to challenge, but not so high to frustrate you; set mini-goals along the way; overall rating of the mobile tool to define goals, set-aside time, bind goals to daily activities, keep track of time invested on each goal, and monitor these analytics (Table 1).

Table 1. Evaluation of the tool with 5-likert scale (5:"strongly agree", 1:"strongly disagree")

Potentials of the tool	SD	AVG
Manage learning goals	0.84	3.36
Foster awareness on preferred learning environments	0.70	3.79
Integrate learning with daily life activities	0.61	3.29
Learn across contexts	0.78	3
Set aside time to learn on regular basis	1	3.07
Adjust goals high enough to challenge but not so high to frustrate you	1.12	3.21
Set mini-goal along the way	0.73	3.93
Overall rating	0.75	3.43

Finally an open discussion was proposed around the following two questions: (1) *"What kind of feedback do you find suitable to be provided with this tool?"*. Tips for productive listening, writing or reading were highlighted as a potential feedback supplied in the form of pushed notifications. E.g. Participant#4 suggested that it might be interesting if she would receive a notification prompting to determine the learning goals before starting the lecture or suggesting tips for productive listening like taking notes or asserting. Participant#7 stressed that notifications prompting to reflect on what has been learned after accomplishing the learning activity could help to make knowledge more persistent. Participant#8 suggested that it would be interesting to rate my perceived productivity after a learning activity and correlate it with the time of the day, day of the week, duration of the task, type of device used or location where I accomplished the learning activity. Participant#3 suggested providing a notification when you should make a break.

A second question 2 proposed a discussion about (2) *"In which learning scenarios do you consider this tool can be applied?"*. Participant#1 suggested extending the scope of the mobile tool from self-regulation to a scenario in formal education. *"Books in secondary school could be NFC-tagged so that the teachers could use this tool to get a grasp on which subjects do students invest more/less time in their homework"*. Participant#9 stressed the importance of the tool for self-awareness *"this tool could help me to establish some limits to the time I invest in non-academic tasks versus the time I invest in academic tasks"*. Participant#3 stated, *"Sometimes you are so tied up with concrete projects that you really need to stop, reflect and organize your learning goals. This tool can be not only used to organize your learning time but also any other daily life activity"*. Upon all these statements, several participants pinpointed to the learning analytics illustrated in Fig. 4 as a very interesting feature to quantify your learning style and become aware of the time devoted to learning activities in long term.

4   Conclusions and Future Work

The observations on the lifelong learning process indicate that typical learning activities of continuing and further education are poorly connected to the daily activities of the learners. There is no support for learning activities across locations, devices and environments and there is a need to provide customized feedback to lifelong learning activities. The tool presented in this manuscript represents an approach to these problems. Tracking when, where and how learning occurs along the day provides rich information to infer lifelong learner's owns habits. This paper reviews previous work on educational scenarios using NFC and four pillars for seamless support of lifelong learners are identified. The NFC LearnTracker has been presented and evaluated as a tool to lead lifelong learners towards a self-regulated process: fostering awareness on learning goals and learning moments; facilitating the user to keep track of learning time with a natural interface; fostering engagement and motivation on the task providing feedback with useful statistics. The Lifelong Learning Hub Project[4] has been released under open licences with the aim to foster its adaptation to further educational communities as well as to facilitate the extension to the increasing number of NFC tags existent in the market.

As limitations, the evaluation of this tool has been performed in an artificial context (Technology Enhanced Learning workshop). The NFC LearnTracker should be tested in longitudinal studies with personal mobile devices and in lifelong learning settings. A realistic scenario must contemplate that the single decision to start using the tool should be triggered by an intrinsic motivation from the user to explore his learning patterns rather than an externally imposed tool. The effects in self-regulation and intrusiveness of logging learning time and monitoring learning patterns should be

---

[4] Lifelong Learning Hub Project site. https://sites.google.com/site/lifelonglearninghubproject/.

explored in further research. This tool might be an interesting approach to determine whether students with more scattered and shorter learning moments are correlated with better or worst performance.

In further research, we will investigate the effects in self-regulation of self-defined internal feedback loops [25] via ambient learning displays [26] based on the patterns identified with the NFC LearnTracker. This feedback will be mapped to the *check-in* and *check-out* events so users can customize and receive stop-and-think signals to reflect when starting a learning activity, doing it or finishing it [27].

The contribution of this manuscript is presenting a tool for lifelong learners to bridge scattered personal learning environments in which learners can define personal ecologies and experience the interaction with such a system in long term typical lifelong learner settings. This research aims at giving an open, flexible and low-cost prototyping framework for defining and linking everyday learning activities to contexts, physical artefacts, everyday home media solutions, and supporting to link sustainable learner tracks to these components.

References

1. Eurostat: Lifelong Learning Statistics (2012)
2. Chan, T.-W., Roschelle, J., Hsi, S., Sharples, M., Brown, T., Patton, C., Cherniavsky, J., Pea, R., Norris, C., Soloway, E., Balacheff, N., Scardamalia, M., Dillenbourg, P., Looi, C.-K., Milrad, M., Hoppe, U.: One-To-One technology-enhanced learning: an opportunity for global research collaboration. Res. Pract. Technol. Enhanc. Learn. **01**, 3–29 (2006)
3. Wong, L.-H., Looi, C.-K.: What seams do we remove in mobile-assisted seamless learning? a critical review of the literature. Comput. Educ. **57**, 2364–2381 (2011)
4. Wong, L.-H.: A learner-centric view of mobile seamless learning. Br. J. Educ. Technol. **43**, E19–E23 (2012)
5. Candy, P., Brookfield, S.: Self-direction for lifelong learning: a comprehensive guide to theory and practice, San Francisco, USA (1991)
6. Tabuenca, B., Ternier, S., Specht, M.: Supporting lifelong learners to build personal learning ecologies in daily physical spaces. Int. J. Mob. Learn. Organ. **7**, 177–196 (2013)
7. Johnson, L., Brown, S., Cummins, M., Estrada, V.: The Technology Outlook for STEM + Education 2012-2017: An NMC Horizon Report Sector Analysis (2012)
8. Ericsson: More than 50 billion connected devices (2011)
9. Specht, M., Tabuenca, B., Ternier, S.: Ubiquitous learning trends in the internet of Things. Campus Virtuales. **2**, 30–44 (2013)
10. Dodson, B., Lam, M.: Micro-interactions with NFC-Enabled Mobile Phones. Mob. Comput. Appl. Serv. **95**, 118–136 (2012)
11. Tabuenca, B., Kalz, M., Specht, M.: Tap it again, Sam: harmonizing the frontiers between digital and real worlds in education. In: Frontiers in Education Conference. IEEE Computer Society, Madrid (2014)
12. Ebner, M., Maierhuber, M.: Near field communication which potentials does NFC bring for teaching and learning materials? Int. J. Interact. Mob. Technol. **7**, 9–14 (2013)
13. Kuflik, T., Stock, O., Zancanaro, M., Gorfinkel, A., Jbara, S., Kats, S., Sheidin, J., Kashtan, N.: A visitor's guide in an active museum. J. Comput. Cult. Herit. **3**, 1–25 (2011)

14. Pérez-Sanagustín, M., Ramírez-González, G., Hernández-Leo, D., Muñoz-Organero, M., Santos, P., Blat, J., Delgado Kloos, C.: Discovering the campus together: a mobile and computer-based learning experience. J. Netw. Comput. Appl. **35**, 176–188 (2012)
15. Kubicki, S., Lepreux, S., Kolski, C.: RFID-driven situation awareness on TangiSense, a table interacting with tangible objects. Pers. Ubiquit. Comput. **16**, 1079–1094 (2011)
16. Ailisto, H., Pohjanheimo, L., Välkkynen, P., Strömmer, E., Tuomisto, T., Korhonen, I.: Bridging the physical and virtual worlds by local connectivity-based physical selection. Pers. Ubiquit. Comput. **10**, 333–344 (2006)
17. Muñoz-Organero, M., Ramírez-González, G., Muñoz-Merino, P.J., Kloos, C.D.: Evaluating the effectiveness and motivational impact of replacing a human instructor by mobile devices for teaching network services configuration to telecommunication engineering students. In: 2010 10th IEEE International Conference on Advanced Learning Technologies, pp. 284–288 (2010)
18. Ramírez-González, G., Córdoba-Paladinez, C., Sotelo-Torres, O., Palacios, C., Muñoz-Organero, M., Delgado-Kloos, C.: Pervasive learning activities for the LMS LRN through android mobile devices with NFC support. In: 2012 IEEE 12th International Conference on Advanced Learning Technologies, pp. 672–673 (2012)
19. Butler, D., Winne, P.: Feedback and self-regulated learning a theoretical synthesis. Rev. Educ. Res. **65**(3), 245–281 (1995)
20. Carroll, J.: Five reasons for scenario-based design. In: Proceedings of the 32nd Hawaii International Conference on System Sciences. IEEE, Hawaii (1999)
21. Tabuenca, B., Kalz, M., Börner, D., Ternier, S., Specht, M.: Where is my time? identifying productive time of lifelong learners for effective feedback services. In: Kalz, M., Ras, E. (eds.) CAA 2014. CCIS, vol. 439, pp. 149–161. Springer, Heidelberg (2014)
22. LAK: 1st international conference on learning analytics and knowledge. In: International Conference on Learning Analytics and Knowledge, p. 2011, Alberta (2011)
23. Siemens, G., Long, P.: Penetrating the fog: analytics in learning and education. Educ. Rev. **46**(5), 31–40 (2011)
24. NXP: NFC Forum Type Tags White Paper (2009)
25. Narciss, S.: Feedback strategies for interactive learning tasks. Handb. Res. Educ. Commun. Technol. **3**, 125–144 (2007)
26. Börner, D., Kalz, M., Specht, M.: Beyond the channel: a literature review on ambient displays for learning. Comput. Educ. **60**, 1–22 (2013)
27. Tabuenca, B., Kalz, M., Ternier, S., Specht, M.: Stop and think: exploring mobile notifications to foster reflective practice on meta-learning. IEEE Trans. Learn. Technol. **8**, 1–12 (2014)

GAMEDUCATION: Using Gamification Techniques to Engage Learners in Online Learning

Mohammad AL-Smadi[✉]

Jordan University of Science and Technology, Irbid, Jordan
maalsmadi9@just.edu.jo

Abstract. Engaging learners long enough to see them through to the end of a course has become one of the most significant problems faced by e-learning developers. The lack of engagement in e-learning can be attributed to three main issues: interaction, challenge and context. Therefore, learning types with high level of interaction and challenge - such as game-based learning – have become widely used. In order to gain the power of games - represented by interaction, motivation, and challenge - e-learning developers started thinking of using game mechanics and dynamics to enhance e-Learning. Gamification of education is still a new trend of research and lacks frameworks and guidelines of how to develop 'gamified' learning tools enabling new forms of engaging learning. This paper reviews theories and research related to learner motivation and engagement. Moreover, it proposes using Gamification in the context of education thus to tackle the lack of learner's engagement.

Keywords: e-Learning · Gamification · Engagement · Motivation

1 Introduction

Learner motivation and engagement has become a challenge to e-learning systems. Therefore, learning types with high level of interaction and challenge - such as game-based learning - have become widely used. The use of games technology for learning is not new and online games have been available for more than a decade. According to Kriz [1], interactive-learning environments foster knowledge transfer, skills and abilities improvement in general and social skills in particular. A variety of educational online games have become available to increase learners' motivation, support collaborative learning and games may foster students to gain knowledge [2].

Despite the benefits of game-based learning and serious games [3–8], the wider adoption of serious games in learning is faced by some challenges and barriers such as the large budget a game needs to be developed [6, 9], the lack of games content specifications thus to be reused in other learning scenarios [5], and the integration with the learning management systems to what and how to learn [10]. Therefore, researchers in domain of technology-enhanced learning started investigating the applicability of the so-called Gamification in designing learning tools and systems.

© Springer International Publishing Switzerland 2015
M. Ebner et al. (Eds): EiED 2014, CCIS 486, pp. 85–97, 2015.
DOI: 10.1007/978-3-319-22017-8_8

This paper sheds the light on the Gamification research field and gives insights from literature on learners' motivation and engagement. The rest of this paper is organized as follows: Sect. 2 discusses limitations and challenges for raising learner's motivation and engagement. Section 3 discusses Gamification of education GAM-EDUCATION based on theories of social learning and motivation. Nevertheless, it provides a set of findings and recommendations for what does GAMEDUCATION mean and how online learning could be enhanced using Gamification. Section 3 provides conclusions and outlook.

2 Learner Motivation and Engagement in Technology-Enhanced Learning

Motivation is considered as essential factor for effective learning. Motivation for learning has been described as the 'engine' that drives teaching and learning [11]. Moreover, according to Bransford et al. [12] motivation affects the time and effort learners plan or consume to learn or to solve problems. Nevertheless, motivation is considered as an important outcome of education [11], thus teaching and learning activities should be carefully designed to promote motivation.

When e-learning first became popular in the early 1990s, cost effectiveness was promoted as its main advantage over traditional methods of instruction. CD-ROMs could be produced cheaply and distributed globally to cater for a high number of users. The introduction of the Internet increased the reach of e-learning systems and many developers rushed to embrace new emerging web technologies. Unfortunately many developers failed to maximize the full potential of such technologies and although they produced systems that appeared attractive, often the content was poor. On the other hand, many researchers argue that students must be meaningfully engaged in the learning resources for effective learning to occur. Engaging learners long enough to see them through to the end of a course has become one of the most significant problems faced by e-learning developers. This lack of engagement in electronic learning content can be attributed to three main issues: interaction, challenge and context (adapted form ALICE[1] project).

- **Interaction**. It is generally agreed that interactivity is a critical factor in the design of e-learning systems. Such interaction directly affects the learner's overall experience and provides motivation to continue in the learning process. Studies researching the effectiveness of e-learning systems highlight the need for immediate feedback, clear short-term goals and better "flow" in moving through the content. The inherent fixed structure of many e-learning systems often fails to provide adequate mechanisms to support interactivity between the user and the system. In many current cases the only interaction available to the learner is to click on the "next" button to step through the material presented.
- **Challenge**. Learners have indicated that unchallenging learning material fails to stimulate them, making the experience unattractive and discouraging progression.

---

[1] ALICE Project: www.aliceproject.eu, last visited March 10th 2013.

As a result, many are reluctant to repeat this experience. Some researchers suggest that effective learning takes place when there is tension between the learner's base knowledge and the gap between the knowledge and skill to be learned. Such tension fosters a sense of curiosity and/or challenge. Motivation can be further enhanced by incorporating clear short-term goals and providing suitable feedback to encourage the learner to continue. Short-term goals help the learner break down a large task into smaller achievable chunks whilst the feedback gained through interaction helps the learner reflect on the learning process and lets them see the consequences of their actions.

- **Context**. Current e-learning design often fails to situate the learner within the context of their course of study and provide them with a sense of orientation. Students have stressed the importance of being able to appreciate the significance of their current progress in relation to the overall goal of the learning material and how their choices may have affected their progress.

  The profile of the modern learner has changed in recent years. With the advent of the so-called "information age" there is an expectation that the workforce will adapt their skills or even change careers to keep in step with technological advancements [13]. This has led to a growing consensus that learning is a lifelong process with many returning to education to retrain. Nevertheless, since the early 1990s, the proliferation of technology means that students have grown up with computers, MP3 players, mobile phones and digital games [14]. The new learner has so different needs that have to be addressed if e-learning is to be successful. Those needs can be summarized as:

- **Empowerment**. The new learner expects to be in control of their learning experience while in a supportive, collaborative and simulative environment. Thus e-learning systems should promote self-directed learning. Unfortunately, many e-learning systems have a linear structure with a single path through the learning material. While this design is cost-effective, the lack of choice reduces control of the learning experience. Research suggests that having such control is more motivating. A suitable balance is required, however, as self-directed study requires high self-efficacy and vulnerable learners often lack the intrinsic motivation to manage their personal learning experience effectively.

- **Social Identity**. Although current e-learning systems allow learners to move at their own pace they isolate them from their peers participating in the same learning process. This inhibits the learning achieved through social interaction and collaboration, with some learners feeling "lost". Research indicates that a sense of belonging to a social group improves motivation and effective learning overall.

- **Authentic Learning Experience**. Learners expect the material to be linked to prior knowledge and be relevant to their everyday lives and careers. In short, the new learner is seeking an "authentic learning experience". Generally, learners are more engaged when they are participating in activities that they can relate directly to prior knowledge and make connections between what they are learning and the real world.

  If such links are missing, learners are less inclined to participate in the learning process and may see it as pointless. For the new generation who are used to customizing their environment there needs to be flexibility in the order and way in which material is studied. Therefore, learning designers have started thinking and looking for tools and ideas to raise learners' engagement and motivation and to provide challenging, contextualized and highly interactive learning tools and objects. Among these ideas is to use the game design thinking in designing online learning.

3   GAMEDUCATION: GAMIFICATION of Technology-Enhanced Learning

Gamification is a new trend of research focusing on using game mechanics and dynamics in non-game contexts to stimulate desired behaviors. Gamification has shown its value in the domain of marketing in particular and other domains such as health, politics, and environment [15]. However, Gamification in education (GAMEDUCA-TION) aims at redesigning e-learning systems to utilize the benefits of game-based learning and serious games to motivate learners to learn better, further engage them, situate their learning, and to maintain their social identity. However, how to 'gamify' e-learning?

Apart from game-based learning, Gamification of education has little research [16]. The mechanics of the game are the actions, behaviors, and controls that are used to 'gamify' an activity in order to (a) stimulate specific emotions on the player (Emotional level), (b) encourage learners to explore, try, and experiment gamified learning setups (Cognition level), and maintain learners social identity through social spaces for learning (Social level), whereas game dynamics are the result of achievements, desires and motivations reflecting activities on those levels (see Table 1).

Table 1. Game mechanics and game dynamics (adapted from [15, 17])

Game mechanics	Game dynamics	Game aesthetics
Points	Reward	Curiosity
Levels	Status	Satisfaction
Challenges	Achievement	Surprise
Virtual goods and spaces	Self-expression	Trust
Leaderboards	Competition	Envy
Gifts and charity	Altruism	Fun

The definition mentioned above highly depends on the MDA framework for game design [17]. MDA stands for Mechanics, Dynamics and Aesthetics as main elements to consider when it comes to design a game. Reference [18] proposes a more generic definition of Gamification as "the use of game design elements in non-game contexts". However, this definition and the MDA framework hold a design challenge of how to design interactions for game design elements that triggers users' desirable emotional responses in order to stimulate target behaviors. Thus, provides meaningful learning that overcomes the quoted problems and limitations in Sect. 2.

3.1 Raising Learner Motivation and Engagement Using Gamification

Raising motivation and providing engaging learning is a major concern for TEL designers as discussed in Sect. 2. This section sheds the light on some theories related to motivation and engagement and how those theories are applied to the domain of Gamification.

Among the motivation theories is the 'Flow' theory, - developed by Csikszentmihalyi's in 1979 - is interested in how an intrinsically rewarding experience feels [19]. From his research and interviews, he has concluded that pure intrinsically motivated behaviors involve enjoyment, complete immersion in the activity, detailed focus, feelings of competence, and loss of conception of time. He stated that the enjoyment from the 'flow' experience further motivates the individual to seek additional challenges. This experience or 'flow' can only result from a situation where high challenges are matched with high skills. A skill/challenge imbalance leads to less than ideal emotional states: *"when challenge is higher than skill, anxiety will be experienced; when challenge is low and skills are high, boredom will result; when both skill and challenge are low, apathy will be experienced."*

Most of us have had that "involved" moment happen, when we concentrated our attention so intensely on solving a problem, reading a book, climbing a mountain, on some task, that we lost track of time and when we became aware of our surroundings, few hours or more had passed by as if they were minutes. Such 'flow', according to Csikszentmihalyi [20] is "optimal experience" that leads to happiness and creativity. Flow is the state in which people are so involved in an activity that nothing else seems to matter; the experience is so enjoyable that people will do it even at great cost, for the sheer sake of doing it. If a task is not challenging enough, boredom sets in, while too challenging task leads to anxiety to happen, and both cases should be avoided. As one's skills increase, then the challenge must also increase for one to remain in a state of flow. Because flow is an enjoyable experience, one continues to increase the challenge level, and consequently continues to improve one's skills because doing so is necessary to stay in a flow state. A learning environment in which students are challenged at an appropriate level, which can produce flow, will be more productive.

Another motivation related model is the Fogg Behavior Model (FBM)[2] through which anticipated user behavior is controlled by three main factors: motivation, ability, and triggers. The FBM model argues that for a target behavior to happen, the user must have sufficient motivation, sufficient ability, and effective trigger. According to FBM, a trigger has different names: cue, prompt, call to action, request, and etc. Moreover, the model defines three types of triggers based on combinations of ability and motivation levels as: spark is a trigger that comes when a user has a high ability to do an action and low motivation to do it whereas the facilitator is associated to high motivation and low

---

[2] http://www.behaviormodel.org/.

ability, and a signal trigger has high ability and high motivation in the same time. However, stimulating a desired behavior requires triggering the user to take an action in the right time when s/he has the sufficient ability and motivation.

Motivation to perform an action can be either intrinsic or extrinsic. Intrinsic motivation is usually happening when the behavior itself satisfies users, where extrinsic motivation is often derived by potential gains such as money, rewards, or praise [11]. The research of [21] shows that there is an evidence of the influence of intrinsic motivation on learners' engagement that leads to 'deep' learning through higher level thinking skills and conceptual understanding. Moreover, Crooks [22] highlights the problems associated with extrinsic motivation as it leads to 'shallow' instead of 'deep' learning. The Self-Determination Theory (SDT) focuses on the degree to which an individual's behavior is self-motivated and self-determined. The theory examines the influence of extrinsic motives on the intrinsic ones for achieving target behaviors. For instance, in an analysis study for 128 studies related to motivation evaluation in education led to that mostly extrinsic motives – i.e. rewards – minimized the level of intrinsic motivations [23]. Nicholson [24] argues that the game design elements used to 'gamify' a service should be rewarding themselves without any need for extrinsic motives and rewards. Moreover, Nicholas accommodates the user-centered design theory in designing interactive objects that foster target behavior. Nevertheless, involving users in the creation and the customization of the game design elements used to 'gamify' a system enables them to self-determine which objects matches their interests.

In the same context, Zang [25] builds on the affordance theory – i.e. action properties for an object actor interaction - and argues that Information and Computer Technology (ICT) should be used based on a "motivational affordances". Motivational affordances deal with including only the objects properties that match the users' needs and interests. Deterding [26] goes further and proposes a conceptual model for designing meaningful game elements for Gamification purposes. The model builds on the SDT and implements the motivational affordances theory in order to achieve meaningful Gamification through extending them with situation and context. Deterding also argues that users are more interested and engaged when they interact with elements that match their interest and fit with their context and background.

Focusing on learners' social identity and social style, it's important to relate our discussion to the theories behind social learning. Bandura's social learning theory (SLT) [27] argues that learning occurs due to interaction with others - i.e., in a social context. Behavior, attitudes, and emotional reactions are developed by observing, imitating, and modeling the behavior of other people. In particular, behavior is more likely to be acquired when the result of this behavior is desirable. Accordingly, there are four processes that underline social learning[3]: attention, retention, motor repro-duction, and motivation. Therefore, one prerequisite of learning is that attention has to be paid to an object or task. Attention is varied by several factors like individual's characteristics (e.g. sensory capacities or arousal level) or complexity. Retention means that it is necessary to remember for what attention was paid. Reproduction means that

---

[3] http://www.learning-theories.com.

the image has to be reproduced, and motivation means that there must be a good reason to imitate the image. Another theory is the social development theory [28] which argues that social interaction plays a fundamental role in the development of cognition. Moreover, Vygotsky argues that the potential for cognitive development depends upon the "zone of proximal development" (ZPD): a level of development attained when learners engage in social behavior. Full development of the ZPD depends upon full social interaction. The range of skill that can be developed with adult guidance or peer collaboration exceeds what can be attained alone.

Social Learning plays major role in defining interactions between objects and avatars in 3D virtual words and serious games. For instance, Smith and Berge [29] investigated the influence of Bandura's SLT in SecondLife[4]. SecondLife is a three-dimensional, virtual world where users are represented by avatars. Smith and Berge suggested that the proposed components of SLT (observing, imitating, and modeling) can also be observed in virtual worlds and that SecondLife is "a great example of social learning theory in action, although there are some components that cannot be satisfied in-world". For instance, it is not possible to observe attitudes and emotional actions in SecondLife. However, cooperation in such learning communities is influenced by the characteristics of its members [30]. Moreover, for emerging a social space, three factors that should be considered: First, there should be *continuity*, meaning that there should be a continuity of contact, members can be recognized, and a historical record of actions. Second, a *community* should be *populated heterogeneously* with all types of members to ensure liveliness of the community. Third, *clear boundaries* and set of rules are required that can be monitored and sanctioned. Such boundaries facilitate cooperation.

Pink [31] defines three main factors for task-performance support: *autonomy*, *mastery*, and *purpose*. In the context of GAMEDUCATION, Pink theory can be applied to education through empowering learners with highly interactive and engaging tools that (a) support learners to be self-directed (autonomy), (b) maintain the learners desire to learn and achieve better results (mastery), and (c) align learning objectives to learner's purpose of learning which in other words aligns the self-directed learning objectives with the curricula objectives.

Based on that, how effectively game design elements can be used to 'gamify' non-game contexts in general and TEL in particular. Apparently Gamification goes beyond using game design elements in non-game contexts to more considering how to apply game design elements in non-game contexts while matching the user interest and background and providing situated and challenging elements. Moreover, when it comes to apply Gamification to TEL, alignment with instruction and learning should be considered. Therefore, using ICT in education requires instructional affordances and learning affordances in addition to motivational affordances. This leads to a question of to what extent available/potential Gamification-based learning platforms use the instructional, learning, and motivational affordances.

Researchers in the domain of Gamification are dealing with similar challenges on how to use game design elements in an effective way to provide meaningful

---

[4] http://secondlife.com.

Gamification. For instance, Nicholson [24] proposes a user-centered theoretical framework for meaningful Gamification through which he is dealing with the user motivation problems. More precisely, the framework tries to solve the problem of negative influence of extrinsic motivation – mainly rewards – on users' intrinsic motivation. The framework leads to define meaningful Gamification as "the integration of user-centered game design elements into non-game contexts". Nicholson argues that involving end users in the creation and customization of the 'gamified' system enables them to select and create meaningful game elements that go in line with their needs and interests.

Kim[5] discusses how to achieve sustainable engagement in Gamification systems. Kim focuses on social engagement form a viewpoint of a game designer by first knowing who play is and what is their social style. Therefore, Kim has adapted Bartle's MUD player types [32] with more emphasis on social styles of the players into *Compete* (similar to Bartle's Achiever), *Collaborate* (similar to Bartle's Socializer), *Explore* (identical to Bartle's Explorer), and *Express* (a replacement for Bartle's Killer). Nevertheless, she uses this adaptation to collect social engagement verbs that can be allocated to each on these four types of players' social styles and used to design Gamification systems (see Fig. 1). Kim also recommends using the PERMA model in designing the engagement loops of the system. The PERMA Model was developed by Martin Seligman in 2011 and aims at supporting human well-being. PERMA stands for the first letters of the model main components as: *Positive Emotion* (experiencing positive emotions such as pleasure, curiosity, etc.), *Engagement/Flow* (moments of consciously involvement in activities), *Positive Relationships* (enjoyable and supportive interactions with others), *Meaning* (creating purposeful narrative), and *Accomplishment/Achievement* (using core values to achieve goals). Kim's work and models hold great promises when it comes to maintain learner social identity in learning environments.

3.2   Findings and Recommendations

Applying Gamification to e-education requires alignment to instruction and learning. Moreover, more focus on learners' social identities and social styles should be taken into account. In order to provide meaningful Gamification in e-education, GAMEDUCATION proposes in addition to situated motivational affordances [26], instructional affordances, learning affordances, and social affordances. Learning affordances comprise the properties of an object that determine whether and how it can support the activity learning type – e.g. collaborative learning, self-directed learning, etc. Instructional affordances include the properties of an object that determine whether and how it can support the instructional design – i.e. e-learning and m-learning. Finally, social affordances include the properties of an object that determine whether and how it can support in maintaining learners social identity and accommodate their social styles. If TEL designers will be able to design learning objects and thus learning tools in a way

---

[5] Smart Gamification, 2011, presentation, http://www.slideshare.net/amyjokim.

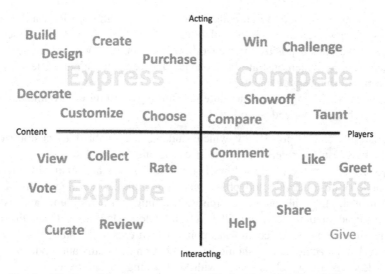

Fig. 1. Kim's social engagement verbs (Kim's Blog: http://amyjokim.com).

that comprise learner needs, interests, and background, moreover to be applied for different learning types and to support different learning approaches then they can contribute to the overcoming of the quoted limitations in TEL and thus provide more engaged learning.

Nowadays no implementation, except for some experiments and attempts limited to single aspects of game elements, is able to offer a complete methodological-techno logical-industrial solution covering the power of games in designing and providing e-learning. Few examples of learning platforms can be found in which game mechanics and dynamics are used to 'gamify' learning. An example of this approach is the Khan Academy[6], a non-profit project providing free materials and resources with the goal of a better education for all. The project's platform includes several game mechanics like achievement badges and points. It also provides up-to-date statistics of students' progress. Moreover, delivered exercises difficulty and challenge cope with the learner skill level as discussed in the flow theory before. Another example is schooools.com, a K-6 social learning environment which is enhanced to encompass games elements based on the social Gamification framework [33].

Examples of using achievements and badges to leverage user behavior on online communities such as the Q&A website Stack Overflow[7] can be found in [33, 35, 36]. Results show that using game dynamics - achievement and badges - increased users' participation and engagement. Similarly, the ResearchGate[8] website where users are assigned a score based on their added publications, Q&A activities, and followers. Research Gate is a social networking site for scientists and researchers to share papers,

---

[6] http://www.khanacademy.org.

[7] StackOverflow provides Q&A support for the programmers: http://stackoverflow.com/.

[8] www.researchgate.net.

ask and answer questions, and find collaborators. User activities on Research Gate can be rated by the research community which then affects their Research Gate score.

Badges have also a positive impact on learners' engagement in online learning [37–40], the research demonstrate how badges and rewards enhanced learners' outcome and raised their engagement.

Consequently, findings form literature on building learning environments that are engaging can be summarized as follows:

- Personalized learner profile, by which students are enabled to customize their avatars based on their personal preferences, belong to social space, and be part of groups. Moreover, the profile allows notifications access and maintains privacy.
- Design learning as levels and phases enabling multiple learning paths, repeated experimentation, problems and exercises. Learning tasks, problems and exercises should be adapted to learner skill level and knowledge state. Once the learner finishes an exercise s/he accumulates points which enable the student to achieve a new level. This achievement should be reflected on his status and updates the rank on the leaderboard which is shared with his learning social space.
- Students should receive rapid feedback cycles which scaffold their learning progress and updates their progression bars in the learning social space. Social recognition and rewards may motivate students, engage them, and improve their social and learning skills.
- Complex learning tasks should be broken into simple tasks, the tasks difficulty should be increased to cope with the learner skill level thus to improve learner expectations on completing the task successfully. Moreover, the learning task should be designed to allow different paths to success. This enables the learner to define personal goals and objectives and select and tries several paths to reach the final goal and achieve her/his personal learning goals. Once the learner accomplishes a complex learning task the system - could be teacher, peers - provides bonuses.
- The system should enable social spaces and stimulates desired behavior and social interaction - like supporting peers, peer-review, providing comments, discussion posts, organizing activity, etc. - by offering badges.
- The system should offer the possibility to exchange points and badges with virtual goods or even receive tickets, trips, or registration discounts - could be tuition fees discount. This will stimulate desired behaviors and more engage learners.
- Learners should be empowered to play different roles and participate in the design of the learning activity as well as assessment forms.
- Learning content and tools should be highly interactive and provides challenging learning tasks that adapts to the learner skill and knowledge state.

4 Conclusion and Outlook

Gamification is a new trend of research which refers to the use of game mechanics and dynamics in non-game contexts to stimulate desired behaviors [16]. Gamification of education (GAMEDUCATION) aims at redesigning e-learning systems to utilize the benefits game design elements in motivating learners to learn better, further engage them, situate their learning, and to maintain their social identity. However, applying Gamification to e-education goes beyond using game design elements in e-education and requires alignment to instruction and learning. Moreover, more focus on learner's social identities and social styles should be considered. Therefore, in order to provide meaningful Gamification in e-education, GAMEDUCATION proposes in addition to situated motivational affordances [26] instructional affordances, learning affordances, and social affordances. More precisely, GAMEDUCATION deals with including only the learning objects properties that match the users' needs and interests, situate their learning, and maintain their social identity.

References

1. Kriz, W.C.: Creating effective learning environments and learning organizations through gaming and simulation design. Simulation and Gaming **34**, 495–511 (2003)
2. Gütl, C.: The support of virtual 3D worlds for enhancing collaboration in learning settings. In: Pozzi, F., Persico, D. (eds.) Techniques for Fostering Collaboration in Online Learning Communities Theoretical and Practical Perspectives, pp. 278–299. IGI Global 2011, Hershey (2010)
3. Prensky, M.: Digital-game based learning. McGraw-Hill, New York (2001)
4. Gee, J.P.: What video games have to teach US about learning and literacy. Palgrave Macmillan, New York (2003)
5. De Freitas, S.: Learning in immersive worlds: a review of game-based learning. JISC e-Learning Programme (2006)
6. Van Eck, R.: Digital game based learning: it's not just the digital native who are restless. Educause Rev. **41**, 16–30 (2006)
7. Klopfer, E., Osterweil, S., Salen, K.: Moving Learning Games Forward: Obstacles, Opportunities and Openness. The Education Arcade. Massachusetts Institute of Technology, Cambridge (2009)
8. McGonigal, J.: Reality is broken: why games make US better and how they can change the world. Penguin Books, New York (2011)
9. Johnson, L., Smith, R., Willis, H., Levine, A., Haywood, K.: The 2011 Horizon Report K-12 Edition. The New Media Consortium, Austin, Texas (2011)
10. Burgos, D., Moreno-Ger, P., Sierra, J.L., Fernández-Manjón, B., Specht, M., Koper, R.: Building adaptive game-based learning resources: the marriage of IMS learning design and <e-Adventure>. Simul. Gaming **39**, 414–431 (2008)
11. Harlen, W.: The role of assessment in developing motivation for learning. In: Gardner, J. (ed.) Assessment and Learning, pp. 61–80. Sage Publications, London (2006)
12. Bransford, J.D., Brown, A.L., Cocking, R.R.: How People Learn. National Academy Press, Washington D.C. (2004)
13. Dochy, F.J., McDowell, L.: Introduction. assessment as a tool for learning. Stud. Educ. Eval. **23**, 279–298 (1997)
14. Prensky, M.: Digital Natives. Digital Immigrants. In On the Horizon **9**(5), 1–6 (2001). NCB University Press
15. Bunchball, Inc. Gamification 101: An introduction to the use of game dynamics to influence behavior (2010)

16. Lee, J., Hammer, J.: Gamification in education: what, how, why bother? Acad. Exch. Q. **15** (2), 1–5 (2011)
17. Hunicke, R., LeBlanc, M., Zubek, R.: MDA: A formal approach to game design and game research. In: Proceedings of AAAI workshop on Challenges in Game, AAAI Press (2004)
18. Deterding, S., Dixon, D., Khaled, R., Nacke, L.: From game design elements to gamefulness: defining "Gamification". In: Proceedings from MindTrek 2011, ACM. Tampere, Finland (2011)
19. Csikszentmihalyi, M.: Optimal Experience. Cambridge University Press, New York (1988)
20. Csikszentmihalyi, M.: Flow: The Psychology of Optimal Experience. Harper and Row, New York (1990)
21. Kellaghan, T., Madaus, G.F., Raczek, A.: The Use Of External Examinations to Improve Student Motivation. AERA, Washington, DC. (1996)
22. Crooks, T.J.: The impact of classroom evaluation practices on students. Rev. Educ. Res. **58** (4), 438–481 (1988)
23. Deci, E., Koestner, R., Ryan, R.: Extrinsic rewards and intrinsic motivations in education: reconsidered once again. Rev. Educ. Res. **71**(1), 1–27 (2001)
24. Nicholson, S.: A User-Centered Theoretical Framework for Meaningful Gamification. Paper Presented at Games + Learning + Society 8.0. Madison, WI, June, 2012
25. Zhang, P.: Motivational affordances: reasons for ICT design and use. Commun. ACM **51** (11), 145–147 (2008)
26. Deterding, S.: Situated motivational affordances of game elements: a conceptual model. In: Presented at Gamification: Using Game Design Elements in Non-Gaming Contexts, A Workshop at CHI 2011(2011b)
27. Bandura, A.: Social Learning Theory. General Learning Press, New York (1977)
28. Vygotsky, L.S.: Mind in Society: The development of higher order psychological processes. Harvard University Press, Cambridge, London (1978)
29. Smith, M., Berge, Z.L.: Social learning theory in Second Life. J. Online Learn. Teach. **5**, 439–445 (2009)
30. Kester, et al.: Enhancing social interaction and spreading tutor responsibilities in bottom-up organized learning networks. In: IADIS International Conference on Web Based Communities, 80–87(2006)
31. Pink, D.H.: Drive: The Surprising Truth about What Motivates Us. Riverhead Books, New York (2011)
32. Bartle, R.: Hearts, clubs, diamonds, spades: players Who suit MUDs. J. MUD Res. **1**, 1 (1996)
33. Simões, J., et al.: A social gamification framework for a K-6 learning platform. Comput. Hum. Behav. **29**, 345–353 (2012). doi:10.1016/j.chb.2012.06.007
34. Anderson, A., Huttenlocher, D.: Steering user behavior with badges. In: Proceedings of the 22nd international conference on World Wide Web, pp. 95–105 (2013)
35. Grant, S., Betts, B.: Encouraging user behaviour with achievements: an empirical study. In: Proceedings of the Tenth International Workshop on Mining Software Repositories (MSR), pp. 65–68 (2013)
36. Easley, D., Ghosh, A.: Incentives, gamification, and game theory: an economic approach to badge design. In: Proceedings of the fourteenth ACM Conference on Electronic Commerce, vol. 1, no. 212, pp. 359–376 (2013)
37. Bista, S., Nepal, S.: Using gamification in an online community. In: 2012 8th International Conference, pp. 611–618 (2012)
38. Denny, P.: The effect of virtual achievements on student engagement. In: Proceedings of the SIGCHI Conference on Human Factors in Computing Systems - CHI 2013, p. 763, 2013

39. Mesquita, M., Toda, A., Brancher, J., do Carmo, R.: Utilizing Gamification concepts tied with Social Networks to support students in programming classes. In: Proceedings of the XV Simposio Internacional ´ de Informatica Educativa ´, pp. 127–132 (2013)
40. Domínguez, A., Saenz-de-Navarrete, J., de-Marcos, L., Fernández-Sanz, L., Pagés, C., Martínez-Herráiz, J.J.: Gamifying learning experiences: practical implications and outcomes. Computers and Education, vol. 63, April 2013, pp. 380-392, ISSN 0360-1315. http://dx.doi.org/10.1016/j.compedu.2012.12.020

Immersive and Emerging Technologies
for Cultural and Digital Heritage

Immersive Installation: "A Virtual St Kilda"

J. McCaffery[✉], S. Kennedy, A. Miller, I. Oliver, A. Watterson, and C. Allison

University of St Andrews, St Andrews, Scotland, UK
jm726@st-andrews.ac.uk
http://openvirtualworlds.org

Abstract. This paper discusses a Virtual Histories project, which developed a digital reconstruction of the St Kilda archipelago. St Kilda is the most western part of the United Kingdom. It is a world heritage site for both built and natural environment. The Virtual St Kilda acted as a focus for the collection and presentation of tangible and intangible cultural heritage. It was on show as an exhibition in the Taigh Chearsabah museum (Fig. 5) located in North Uist Scotland. The exhibition is built around the OpenSimulator Open Virtual World server, using commodity hardware. The simulation covers some 4 square km of virtual space, and models both tangible and intangible culture. It is integrated into the exhibition, which articulates an interpretation of the St Kilda legacy through the prism of contemporary North Uist life.

Keywords: Virtual worlds · Museum studies · Immersive technology · Cultural heritage · Reconstruction · Community involvement · Opensim

1 Introduction

This paper discusses the use of Open Virtual World Technology to create an immersive museum exhibit of the St Kilda world heritage site. The exhibit has been enjoyed by thousands of people at the Taigh Chearsabhagh Museum and Arts Centre. It includes a 3D interactive model of St Kilda as it was in the late 19th century. The model is based upon archaeological evidence (Emery 1996, Stell and Harman 1988, Harm 1996) and provides an accurate portrayal of both the geography and architecture of the Village Bay area of Hirta the largest island of the St Kilda archipelago.

St Kilda is an archipelago about 40 miles west of the outer Hebrides, in Scotland. It is both the most western and the remotest land in the British Isles. Evidence has shown that St Kilda's history goes back at least as far as the bronze age. St Kilda's remoteness makes it unique. The culture that developed there over the millennium during which it was inhabited is like no other culture in Britain. Similarly the natural life on the island is also a breed apart, literally in some cases. There are species of birds and mammals on St Kilda found nowhere else. St Kilda is a place of great, if rugged, beauty. It is sheer rock rising out of the Atlantic, the last bit of land before you hit America. All these factors make it a place of fascination for many. It has been designated a UNESCO world

© Springer International Publishing Switzerland 2015
M. Ebner et al. (Eds): EiED 2014, CCIS 486, pp. 101–113, 2015.
DOI: 10.1007/978-3-319-22017-8_9

Fig. 1. Panoramic view of Virtual St Kilda main street

heritage site for both its natural and cultural value. It is one of only twenty four such dual sites in the world and the only one in Scotland. As St Kilda is such a remote site, requiring a four hour boat journey from the Outer Hebrides, few of the many who wish to visit will ever get to go there. The interest it generates and the difficulty of visiting it in person make it an interesting topic for a digital exploration.

The goal of this project was to make such an exhibit using open source software and commodity hardware. For this to work the exhibit had to be easy to use, reliable and capture the scale of the environment. The exhibit was to be unmanned, therefore visitors had to be able to walk up and use it without training. The exhibit also had to run reliably for months without intervention, save being turned on and off at night. A key aspect of St Kilda is the size of the cliffs and surrounding hills and the relationship between human habitation, agricultural architecture and natural environment. To capture this a model which represented several square km of real space was required. Further the exhibit was to integrate the many songs and stories which make up St Kilda's rich culture.

2   The St Kilda Archipelago

The archipelago consists of five islands (Soy, Boneray, Dun, Levenish and Hirte) and several sea stacks, including the highest stack on the British isles. Hirte, the only inhabited island was evacuated in 1930. Villagers lived on the only street on the island (Fig. 1), located on Village Bay. This street, known simply as 'The Street' is lined with crofts, Blackhouses (traditionally Hebridean dwellings with thick walls and doors facing away from the sea) and Cleits (dry stone storage structures, unique to St Kilda, which cover the St Kildan landscape, more than 1100 in total). Village Bay is the closest thing Hirte has to a safe landing. Even in modern times poor weather makes it impossible for boats to offload cargo. When the island was still inhabited the islanders would sometimes go months, or whole winters, without receiving supplies from the mainland. All the factors that make St Kilda special also make it an excellent subject for a reconstruction. Its striking geography is something that can be hard to translate in still images or videos, but translates well into being explored virtually. Due to its remoteness

Fig. 2. Virtual and real views of St Kilda, across village bay, looking out towards Dun.

visitors are unlikely to be able to experience it themselves. The stories that are linked to it interesting strike a universal chord.

The St Kilda model was developed in the first half of 2014. It is a technically challenging model, spanning 4 square km. This is orders of magnitude larger than is normal in OVW models. In order to support the larger size the client was modified to extend the far clipping plane of the view frustum. This enabled views that span from village bay out to the easily recognisable outline of Dun, to the south (Fig. 2). Extending the visible area to include this greatly increases the sense of presence and ensures that the iconic vistas of St Kilda can be recognised immediately. The terrain data is taken from Ordinance Survey GIS information. The reconstruction covers village bay with objective to represent enough of the space such that, when standing in the centre of the village visitors get an accurate impression of the geography in all directions. Modelling focussed on the village itself, here the crofts, Blackhouses and Cleits are all modelled. The models for the Blackhouses and Cleits were developed in external modelling software. This allowed the same models to be used to create high fidelity images and videos using special effect software and used again as imported meshes in the interactive reconstruction.

The model is dated to the 1880s. The reconstruction has been augmented with a number of NPCs. Records from St Kilda are relatively complete so each NPC is named after a real inhabitant of village bay and their appearance taken from contemporary photographs. The model also features embedded content displayed as web pages. Throughout the model there are items which contain further information, which glow when the avatar approaches. When clicked on the viewer's inbuilt web browser displays a web page with text and images presenting information linked to the glowing object.

3 Development Process

The development of Virtual St Kilda was a collaborative process featuring an artist at the University of St Andrews (Sarah Kennedy), expert advice from the National Trust for Scotland (who manage St Kilda) and Access Archaeology, a community archaeological group on North Uist. Once the model was developed supporting material was produced by collaborators, local and national.

The first stage was to use GIS data to create the landscape in which reconstructions would sit. In St Kilda this is particularly important as the shape of the land is one of the most recognisable aspects of the site. The GIS data used is the Ordinance Survey high resolution data.

Fig. 3. External view of Manse and Internal view of Blackhouse model.

For the site to feel authentic accurate reproduction is vital. With the GIS landscape loaded measurements from the site were used to map out the location of every structure to be modelled. These measurements include Google Satellite view data, contemporary accounts and photographs and archaeological surveys. The site as it stands today is relatively unchanged. Several of the crofts have lost their roofs and there is now a modern base, but otherwise the structures stand where they have stood since 1880. Having plotted the location of each structure surviving evidence of the site is surveyed as material to be integrated into the model. As part of this process areas of particular interest, recognisability or iconic status were identified. The date for the reconstruction is within the photographic era. Despite this there are still areas where no direct evidence is available showing precisely how it was in the past. In these instances more general evidence such as equivalent sites and written reports can be used to create an estimate at how that part of the model should look. As the model was developed there were meetings with experts from the National Trust for Scotland, and with members of the Access Archaeology group in Uist, to gather feedback. These meetings allowed expert interpretation to be incorporated into the development process. It is often the case that the ability to view an artefact, building or other element in its natural situation will allow theories to be tested and plausibility evaluated (Getchell et al., 2010). As changes are relatively simple to make multiple different versions of the same feature can be created and experts use these to make a decision about what is most likely to be correct. In this way the iterative design cycle of the Open Virtual World platform enables research into the heritage aspects of the projects. The outside of the manse church complex and the inside of the manse parlour are shown in Fig. 3. Views of NPCs inside a typical 1880 s house and crops growing are shown in Fig. 4. The

Fig. 4. View of cale growing in village bay and residents in past 1830 cottage.

system architecture used to support this development is dicussed in some detail in McCaffery et al., (2013) and an expansion of the reconstruction methodology can be found in Kennedy et al., (2013).

Once the model is created it is populated with content to help those who interact with it learn about the topic. This means adding multi media content and Non Player Characters. The model in turn is raw material that can be integrated into traditional media such as videos and still images, which can be distributed online or included in papers, newspaper articles and informational posters.

A set of videos was created as part of a program of community involvement. North Uist's links to St Kilda mean there is a wealth of material about the archipelago in the community. Many of the islanders have travelled to St Kilda and the video and images they brought back were made available for the project. Images shot on St Kilda were used to make posters for the exhibit and as part of the embedded web pages. Two separate Uist organisations, Uist Film and Island Voices, had produced films about St Kilda. The footage in these films formed the majority of the live action footage which was integrated with virtual footage to produce short videos about St Kilda. The rest of the footage was filmed as part of the project. In order to do this the Kilda Cruises organised a voyage to Hirte. Once there Qinetiq, the contractors who run the base, made transport available so that footage could be shot all over the island in a short space of time. Local groups of musicians from North Uist, including the Gaelic singing teacher for the area, a ceilidh band group known as the Spring Chickens and children at local primaries, recorded pieces related to St Kilda, used in the videos. In the same primary schools pupils researched St Kilda and wrote narratives telling the stories they related to about their far flung neighbour. The childrens' tellings of these stories were recorded and combined with virtual footage and the other material gathered to tell some personal tales with a distinct North Uist voice. Community produced content was combined with National Trust for Scotland archive footage to illustrate some of the more historical aspects of the site. Technology students at a local college produced posters which advertise the exhibit. The National Trust also provided access to a recording of an interview with one of the last inhabitants of village bay. This interview was combined

Fig. 5. Taigh Chearsabhagh Museum and Arts Centre and Virtual St Kilda Exhibition.

with virtual footage and footage supplied by local groups to create videos telling another form of story about life on St Kilda (https://vimeo.com/98057417).

Products of the community engagement include videos available online, streamed into the model and part of the St Kilda exhibit. These videos, as well as the posters that were produced and also the many events that were used to gather the material and share it with the community, help extend the reach of the project in directions that complement the model itself and ensure value in multiple contexts.

Records exist of who lived in what house during the time period. Linked with these names are historical documents photographs. Using this data NPCs were created to represent real inhabitants. These NPCs are scripted to walked through the town, performing the activities that would have filled the islanders days. These NPCs can interact with the user, they can speak, both in audio clips and through text. The research for the NPCs was helped by local knowledge, and by the National Trust for Scotland.

4   The Exhibition Space and Exhibit

The room in which the exhibit is installed is a large, barn like space within the museum. The room is a cuboid space approximately 5 m across, 15 m deep and 6 m high. There is no ceiling, just the beams which support the roof. The door is situated on the front wall, opposite the mezzanine balcony. The installation consists of a 3 × 1 m poster along one wall, a projection covering the width of the front wall, coming down low enough to cover some of the door, a table with a 25" monitor and an XBox controller. The table is overlooked by a Kinect. Everything is controlled by a computer on the mezzanine level. This connects to a projector creating the projection and a wireless received for the XBox controller. The monitor receives its signal through a wireless HDMI kit. A powered USB cable runs from the mezzanine down to the Kinect.

The exhibit itself is made up of a series of short videos, ranging from two to ten minutes long, and a free exploration mode where the visitor uses the XBox controller to explore the model. The videos are intended as short, stand-alone pieces. They are designed with reference to the youtube format, where information is presented in small sections but linked with more information so

Fig. 6. Instructions and main menu of the exhibit.

interested users can explore further if they wish. The videos are discussed above and cover subjects such as health on the islands (https://vimeo.com/100323053), what Blackhouses and Cleits are and recordings of music with known links to St Kilda. There are also two longer videos. The first, 'Impressions of St Kilda (https://vimeo.com/94653938) is a seven minute piece composed of a mix of real world footage and virtual footage introducing St Kilda and the different aspects that make it special and some information about the exhibit. The video has a voiceover narration. Each paragraph of information is narrated first in Gaelic and then English. The second long video is a ten minute long mood piece of the sights and sounds of St Kilda. This is designed to run when visitors have not started interacting with the system at all.

The Blackhouse (https://vimeo.com/94504484) and Cleit (https://vimeo.com/99984295) videos combine renders, done using special effects software, with real world footage, shots from the main model and recordings of local residents performing St Kildan songs. The special effects shots integrate animated text and effects, such as smoke, into a high polygon mesh of the structure (Fig. 5). The high poly meshes were then simplified and imported into the model. The modelling of the Cleits and Blackhouses was done by Alice Watterson and the animation by Alice Watterson and Keiran Baxter. The videos which tell general stories of St Kilda combine virtual footage and real footage. In these videos a static backdrop shot was filmed in the virtual world. Pupils from the local Cairnish primary school were recorded, twice, telling stories they had researched and written out about St Kilda. The first recording was audio only to get a clear recording. In the second a projector was used to cast shadows of the pupils over a white backdrop. This shadow footage was later manipulated in Blender to produce a pure black and white mask of their shadow. The final composite features the children's audio and their shadow projected over the virtual background. A frame from one of these stories is shown in Fig. 7.

Shots of the interactive model used in the Blackhouse and Cleit videos, as well as in the 'Guided Tour', are more dynamic than the static backgrounds of the stories. Camera movements are programmed and then played back using the sofware which powers the exhibit (McCaffery et al., 2014). As they are played back the video stream from the computer is routed through an external device that can capture the stream to an SSD drive and simultaneously patch it

Fig. 7. A frame from the lady grange story. Students explore in stereoscopic 3D.

forward to an output device. When camera movement is introduced lower framerate become readily apparent. The video is recorded at 30FPS so if the client is rendering fewer frames than this output smoothness is jeopardised. Another problem encountered in moving shots is tearing as the camera pans. To solve these challenges the camera moves at 10 % or 1 % of the intended speed of the final movement. This results in many frames of recorded material covering a single frame of intended output. When the footage is sped up again samples across these multiple frames produce a much smoother final image than recording at full speed. This process produces smooth shots without the necessity of reducing graphical options to achieve an optimal framerate. To work all dynamic movement in the scene had to be slowed. This meant adapting scripts which make waves crash, birds circle and smoke sputter to operate at a reduced frequency and not appear hyperactive on the sped up footage.

The exhibit is designed to run without the presence of a member of staff. When the first visitor of the day enters the room the exhibit is playing the mood piece on a loop. This remains until the visitor either moves to the back of the room or starts to press buttons on the XBox controller. When presence is detected in the room by a Microsof Kinect the Guided Tour is played. Once this has completed a notification appears telling the visitor that if they wish to explore further they can pick up the XBox controller and go to the menu. If they do not do this the Blackhouse video plays, followed by one of the recorded songs set to real world footage of St Kilda. Once this has completed the visitor is again prompted to engage with the XBox controller. If they do not more content is presented automatically. After a third prompt the exhibit will go back to playing the mood piece. If at any point the user does engage with the XBox controller they can press a button to go to the main menu. From the main menu, shown in Fig. 6, they access all of the content in the model. To do so they use the joysticks on the XBox controller to move a cursor. When the cursor is hovered over a menu item for a couple of seconds that menu item is selected. Most menu items are made up of several videos, played back to back. Special cases are the option to explore the world directly and the credits. As well as prompts on the screen the exhibit also features laminated signs, instructing the visitor how to control it with the XBox controller. While the exhibit is generally designed not

Fig. 8. A frame from the Cleit animation and render of the inside of a blackhouse

to require staff intervention members of staff will occasionally go into the exhibit and give tours of the content. In these tours they can highlight areas of interest to specific visitors and tailor the experience to the group. This format also means that visitors who might be put off by having to engage with technology can have a more directed experience than simply watching the automated content play (Fig. 8).

A core design principle is community involvement. North Uist is a remote island with a relatively small population. Many people on the island have direct connections to St Kilda. Some have links to the people who once lived there, others work, or have worked there. In order for the exhibit to be received well and integrate into the environment where it was intended to be installed it was very important the local population took ownership of the project. The footage shot by local groups, recordings of local musicians and videos of local primary school students telling stories of St Kilda features centrally in the videos. Taken together this means that the exhibit is a combination of documentary and interpretation. Local, historical, academic and virtual all combine together to create something which is multi-faceted and tells the story of a unique place in a unique way all through a strong local voice. The end result is something that the community is happy to publicise to the world as their perspective on a site of international interest.

5 St Kilda in Schools

As well as installing the St Kilda scene as museum exhibit it was used as the basis for workshops across North and South Uist and Benbecula, known collectively as the 'Long Island'. These islands are three of Scotland's outer Hebrides. Workshops were done in three primary schools and in an adult learning centre. Two of the schools (Lochmaddy and Cairnish, both on North Uist, Fig. 9) were primary schools with only a few dozen students across the 7 primary classes. The third was a larger primary school on Benbecula where students were streamed into Gaelic and English classes. In all schools a computer was set up with a projector and an XBox controller that pupils could gather round and watch content on.

Fig. 9. Pupils in Lochmaddy and Cairnish engage with the content.

In Lochmaddy one group, consisting of the older classes at the school, attended the exhibit. In Cairnish the pupils were split into two groups, younger and older. In both schools the pupils had been involved in the creation of the content and where excited to see themselves projected on the screen. Sessions in Lochmaddy and Cairnish started by showing the 'Guided Tour' video, to introduce the material, and then showing the footage that the children had been involved in the creation of. Having seen the linear material the projector was switched to showing the virtual world and the children were given the opportunity to use the XBox controller to explore St Kilda. When exploring the children were prompted to take turns with the XBox controller, with all children not currently in control able to watch the projection and talk amongst themselves and to the child in control. This process was allowed to be relatively free, pupils were not forced to stay quiet and watch passively, they were encouraged to talk amongst themselves and to commentate on their experience. This lead to very enthusiastic sessions with much laughter and interaction. Pupils enjoyed being able to fly, especially when the ability to cease flying and watch the avatar fall from a height down to the ground was discovered. One of the consistent things that pupils enjoyed was attempting to find unexpected parts of the scene. Exploring underwater or trying to get inside houses which they were not supposed to enter.

In Benbecula primary 6 students visited the workshop, split between the Gaelic and the English streams. Where the settings in Lochmaddy and Cairnish were relatively informal in Benbecula larger class sizes and older students required more structure. In Benbecula each class sat down and watched the 'Guided Tour' video. Having watched the video they were split into two groups, with each group given access to a computer running the scene. In the groups pupils were encouraged to explore and think about questions such as 'How many people do you think lived in the village?' and 'What do you think it might have been living in such a remote place?'. Pupils were encouraged to share control such that everyone had a turn in charge of the avatar. After approximately twenty minutes the groups were relaxed and pupils had the opportunity to try out the Oculus rift. When pupils were initially given control there was some hesitance as to what they should be doing. All groups did explore the scene thoroughly. When the groups were relaxed and some pupils went to try the rift the noted tendency was for those to remain to focus more closely on the scene. Smaller groups lead to those with particular interests getting longer to investigate and familiarise themselves with the content.

Mairi Morrison from Comann Eachdraidh Uibhist a Tuath (North Uist Cultural Society) offered the following reflections: To begin with I had only a vague idea of what we were expected to do. Something about St. Kilda? so when the team arrived they could film some drama and song. With little time to plan, we embarked on our journey of exploration. We had half a morning for five weeks to research and prepare. We decided we would show the DVD of the St. Kilda Story (1980), with footage from 1906 to 1930, and the Wildlife of St Kilda, filmed over 27 years from 1957.

The filming itself, though nerve wracking for some, worked really well, in spite of the scanty preparation. The crew were highly sensitive to the needs of individual children and worked in an enabling way. The ability the process allowed for multiple takes was a distinct advantage, since the children could pause to recollect their words or be prompted. In addition, filming the soundtrack separately in a better acoustic space helped them to relax more and focus on conveying the words and narratives more clearly.

When the children had the opportunity to see the virtual St Kilda and try out the handsets and the 3D goggles for themselves the following day, the effects were startling. They seemed to master the technology, on the whole, swiftly and competently and were mesmerised and enchanted by the opportunities it gave them for movement, visualisation and imagination as they travelled through an unfamiliar terrain and yet a tangible world. Their feedback was instantaneous and heartfelt. Awesome, Its the best thing ever, It feels like youre really there. Educationally it was utterly uplifting. Some pedagogical observations:

1. The medium of media is arresting and exciting- a valuable learning incentive
2. Where the children have ownership of their contributions, they tend to develop personal and group confidence
3. Challenging them with original primary, adult resources helps them to raise their game
4. Careful scaffolding of the learning helps individuals to progress to their next proximal zone (Vygotsky)
5. Working towards a real outcome helps the learning to be more purposeful and relevant
6. Assuming a role reduces the pressure of performing as oneself

The Education Scotland Report, Inspection of the learning community surrounding Sgoil Lionacleit Eilean Siar Council comments: *The Virtual St Kilda Exhibition, codeveloped with children from a local primary school and adult volunteers from the North Uist Historical Society provides very good outcomes related to the four capacities[1] in Curriculum for Excellence.*

---

[1] succesful learners, confident individuals, responsible citizens, effective contributors.

6 Conclusion

This paper has described the creation of the Virtual St Kilda Exhibition. The exhibition provides insight into the lives of people who lived there in the 1880s. It enables appreciation of the relationship between the natural environment and human habitation, In doing so it enables visitors to make use of existing digital literacies to explore the past. Through using commodity hardware and open-source software it has been possible to create an exhibit which captures both intangible culture the stories, songs and lives of the inhabitants and material culture the buildings and artefacts. In addition to the positive outcomes of the development process, the exhibition itself has been well received. When the Virtual St Kilda exhibit opened visitor numbers are up by 28 % compared to the previous year. Feedback from visitors to the exhibit has been positive.

References

Jemni, M.A., Driss, Z., Kantchev, G., Abid, M.S.: Intake manifold shape influence on the unsteady in-cylinder flow: application on LPG bi-fuel engine. In: Haddar, M., Romdhane, L., Louati, J., Ben Amara, A. (eds.) Design and Modeling of Mechanical Systems. LNME, vol. 1, pp. 331–338. Springer, Heidelberg (2013)

Dawson, T., Vermehren, A., Miller, A., Oliver, I., Kennedy, S.: Digitally enhanced community rescue archaeology. In: Digital Heritage International Congress (Digital-Heritage) 2013, vol. 2, pp. 29–36 (2013)

Dow, L., Campbell, A., Miller, A., McCaffery, J., Davies, C.J., Kennedy, S.: An immersive platform for collaborative projects. In: Proceedings of the Frontiers in Education Conference FIE 2014, Madrid, Spain. IEEE (2014)

Emery, N.: Excavations of Hirta 1986–90. HMSO, Edinburgh (1996)

Getchell, K., Miller, A., Allison, C., Sweetman, R.: Exploring the second life of a byzantine basilica. In: Petrovic, O., Brand, A. (eds.) Serious Games on the Move, pp. 165–180. Springer, Vienna (2009)

Getchell, K., Miller, A., Nicoll, J.R., Sweetman, R., Allison, C.: Games methodologies and immersive environments for virtual fieldwork. IEEE Trans. Learn. Technol. 3(4), 281–293 (2010)

Harman, M.: An Isle Called Hirte. MacLean Press, Skye (1996)

Kennedy, S.E., Fawcett, R., Miller, A.H.D., Sweetman, R.J., Dow, L., Campbell, A., Oliver, I.A., McCaffery, J.P., Allison, C.: Exploring canons and cathedrals with open virtual worlds: the recreation of st andrews cathedral, st andrews day, 1318. In: Proceedings of UNESCO Congress on Digital Heritage. IEEE (2013)

Klein, R., Santos, P. (eds.): Eurographics Workshop on Graphics and Cultural Heritage. Eurographics Association, Darmstadt, Germany (2014)

McCaffery, J., Miller, A., Oliver, I.: Measurement of immersive technology for historic scenes. In: Klein, R., Santos, P. (eds.) Eurographics Workshop on Graphics and Cultural Heritage, pp. 107–116 (2014)

McCaffery, J.P., Miller, A.H.D., Kennedy, S.E., Vermehren, A., Lefley, C., Strickland, K: Exploring heritage through time and space: supporting community reflection on the highland clearances. In: Proceedings of UNESCO Congress on Digital Heritage. IEEE (2013)

Oliver, I., Miller, A., Allison, C.: Mongoose: throughput redistributing virtual world. In: Computer Communications and Networks (ICCCN) 2012, 21st International Conference on, pp. 1–9 (2012)

Oliver, I.A., Miller, A.H.D., Allison, C.: Virtual worlds, real traffic. In: Proceedings of the First Annual ACM SIGMM Conference on Multimedia systems - MMSys 2010, p. 305, New York, USA. ACM Press (2010)

Stell, G.P., Harman, M.: Buildings of St Kilda. HMSO, Edinburgh (1988)

Mobile Exploration of Medieval St Andrews

Adeola Fabola, Chris Davies, Sarah Kennedy, Alan Miller^(⊠),
and Colin Allison

School of Computer Science, University of St Andrews, St Andrews, UK
alan.miller@st-andrews.ac.uk

Abstract. Saint Andrews is a town with a rich history. It was the religious centre of Scotland for close to a millennium. The Cathedral was strongly associated with the wars of Independence and Robert the Bruce. The castle was the scene of pivotal revolt leading to the reformation and hosted the first Scottish protestant congregation. St Salvators Chapel was the religious centre of Scotland's first University. This paper presents work which explores using mobile technologies to support investigation, learning and appreciation of the past. It builds on tradition and world class scholarship into the history of this important town and makes them available to school students, researchers and tourists using mobile technologies. From text based quests, through mobile apps to location aware stereoscopic 3D experiences the gamut of available commodity and emerging hardware is used to enable the past to be explored in new ways.

1 Introduction

Exploration of the past is often seen as a dry subject to be conducted with dusty tombs in dark libraries. Yet the widespread use of mobile and increasingly immersive technologies mean that new generations are more literate in the manipulation of digital data than ever before. These technologies and literacies can be put to use both to provide new insights into the past and to communicate established scholarship in ways that are accessible and engaging to new audiences.

The work described in this paper extends a Virtual Time Travel Platform (VTTP) (McCaffery et al. 2013) to support exploration of the past on mobile devices. The VTTP supports both the creation and deployment of 3D digital reconstructions of historical scenes. It is based on Open Virtual World Technology and has been engineered (Oliver et al. 2010, Oliver et al. 2012, Oliver et al. 2013, McCaffery et al. 2014) to support real time interaction in large scale high fidelity environments using open source software and commodity hardware.

The reconstructions are based upon archaeological (Dawson et al. 2013) and historical evidence (Fawcett 2011, Fawcett et al. 2003, Fawcett and Rutherford 2011). They model not just the physical scenes but tangible and intangible culture, both the fixtures and fittings of everyday life and the people together with their work, songs and stories. They enable engaging learning environments to be created which make sue of digital literacies developed playing games (Getchell et al. 2010).

This platform has formed the basis of installations in Museums, for example a reconstruction of the Scottish highland Caen township in the Timespan Museum

© Springer International Publishing Switzerland 2015
M. Ebner et al. (Eds): EiED 2014, CCIS 486, pp. 114–124, 2015.
DOI: 10.1007/978-3-319-22017-8_10

and Arts Centre. It has been used to enable school students at Madras college to explore reconstructions of the local St Andrews Cathedral, has been used in higher education degrees in the arts (Getchell et al. 2009), social science (Ajinomoh et al. 2012) and the sciences (McCaffery et al. 2014) and is accessible over the Internet (Dow et al. 2014). In (Davies et al. 2013) a virtual time window system is described where mobile devices present a window into the past.

This paper presents and compares three modes of interacting with the past, and their supporting technologies. The QuestIt system guides a visitor through medieval St Andrews using texts sent and received by a mobile phone. Texts provide an intimate yet low fi form of communication accessible to all.

The location aware app provides a framework which enables both onsite and offsite exploration of St Andrews. Digital reconstructions, contemporary drawings and maps are combined with modern commentary and views. Blending, text, images, audio and video with panoramas, 3D objects and links to immersive scenes enables multiple digital interpretations of the subjects to be accessed whilst exploring the sites.

The Mirrorshades systems enables a Stereoscopic Head Mounted Display (SHMD), to simultaneously present views of the real world and a parallel virtual world. The users realworld view is synchronized with the Virtual World view using location and orientation tracking. This enables digital models to be appreciated in stereoscopic 3D and be simultaneously compared with the modern site. We describe the reconstruction of St Salvators chapel and its exploration using the Mirrorshades system.

We believe that the three modes of interaction are complementary to each other. Stereoscopic headsets provide a high quality immersive experience, text quests provide engagement and the app provide onsite access to multi-media context. Taken together they have the potential to revolutionise the way we interact with the past.

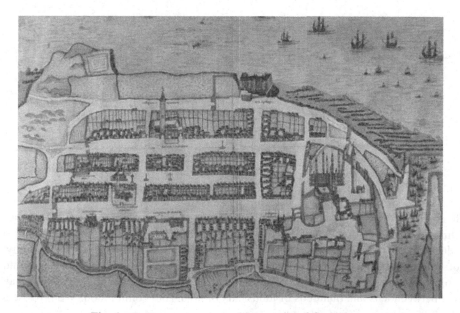

Fig. 1. Contemporary view of late medieval St Andrews

2   Overview of Mediaeval St Andrews Mobile Learning App

This project brings together computer science, history and archaeology academics and students to create a Mediaeval St Andrews app. The Medieval St Andrews app will enable learners to concurrently explore the physicality of St Andrews and access location specific research. The app acts as a guide providing a narrative linking together specific locations on the physical trail. This encourages self-paced student centred learning. For each point of interest on the trail text, images, audio and video, combine with the physicality of the location to provide an engaging learning experience that motivates further reflection. Links to online digital resources, which index relevant scholarly research guide further investigation. In this way new research learning linkages are created.

Smart phones and tablets are becoming ubiquitous and have the functionality to add a new dimension to learning. They typically contain GPS, a high resolution screen and connect to the Internet. The Mediaeval St Andrews App enables the synthesis of scene and discourse in the learning process. Until now the cost of app authoring has been too high for this technology to be integrated into infrastructure of learning in higher education. This project demonstrates the educational value of integrating location into the learning process and has developed a framework for educational app creation.

St Andrews is a town central to Scottish and world history (Fig. 1). Robert the Bruce attended the consecration of St Andrews Cathedral (Fig. 4), whilst the diocese funded him through the wars of independence. St Salvators dates from the foundation of Scotland's first University (Figs. 9, 10, 11, 12). St Andrews was a driving force for the reformation with the Castle being home to Scotland's first protestant congregation. Evidence of this rich history is interwoven with the fabric of the town.

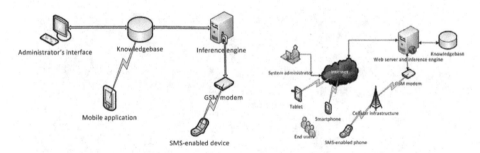

Fig. 2. QuestIt system design   **Fig. 3.** Conceptual architecture

There is a rich potential for further location aware learning apps. Within St Andrews: History of the University, Witches Tour, the Books of St Andrews, Churches of St Andrews and History of Golf are examples. This approach is also valuable across disciplines with relevance in history, art history, classics and divinity, location aware apps will also enhance virtual fieldwork in geography, geo-science and ecology. The design and creation of apps currently attracts a premium. Single apps may cost between tens and hundreds of thousands of pounds to commission. We propose a

Fig. 4. Reconstruction of St Andrews cathedral 1318

generic format, abstracted from existing apps, which will support multiple disciplines and applications.

A welcome page with embedded photograph and image map provides a visually striking introduction. At the heart of each app is a zoomable interactive map. A user's location and clickable points of interest are represented. Each point of interest may have text, images, audio, video, a 3D panorama and a 3D model associated with it. These stimulate interest and act as gateways pointing to further learning and research materials.

We have designed a web user interface which enables app content to be easily created and updated. A simple form enables upload of the images, audio, video and text associated with each site. The live map area is defined in latitude/longitude coordinates, if required a custom map may be uploaded. Points of interest are defined by entering latitude/longitude coordinate pairs. Each point of interest is then associated with text, images, audio and video as appropriate. This interface enables students to create apps enabling co-curriculum development of communication skills and engagement with professional publication issues. Once the content for the app is defined open source tools allow automatic compilation for iOS, Android and other platforms.

This project draws upon scholarship and student input in the schools of History, Art History and Classics. It marries the teaching and research agendas of staff in the Institute of Mediaeval Studies (SAIMS) and in the Institute of Scottish Historical Research (ISHR) which supports the umbrella project and teaching portfolio of Mediaeval St Andrews. It will make accessible reconstructions of historic St Andrews structures notably the St Andrews Cathedral (https://vimeo.com/77928887), St Andrews Castle and St Salvators chapel.

2.1 Texting

This section discusses the considerations and activities that went into the design phase of the system. There are two main user groups for the system: System Administrators: These are computer-literate staff of cultural heritage organisations. They will interact with the system through a web interface that provides functionality to populate the knowledgebase with heritage information as well as additional features to modify this

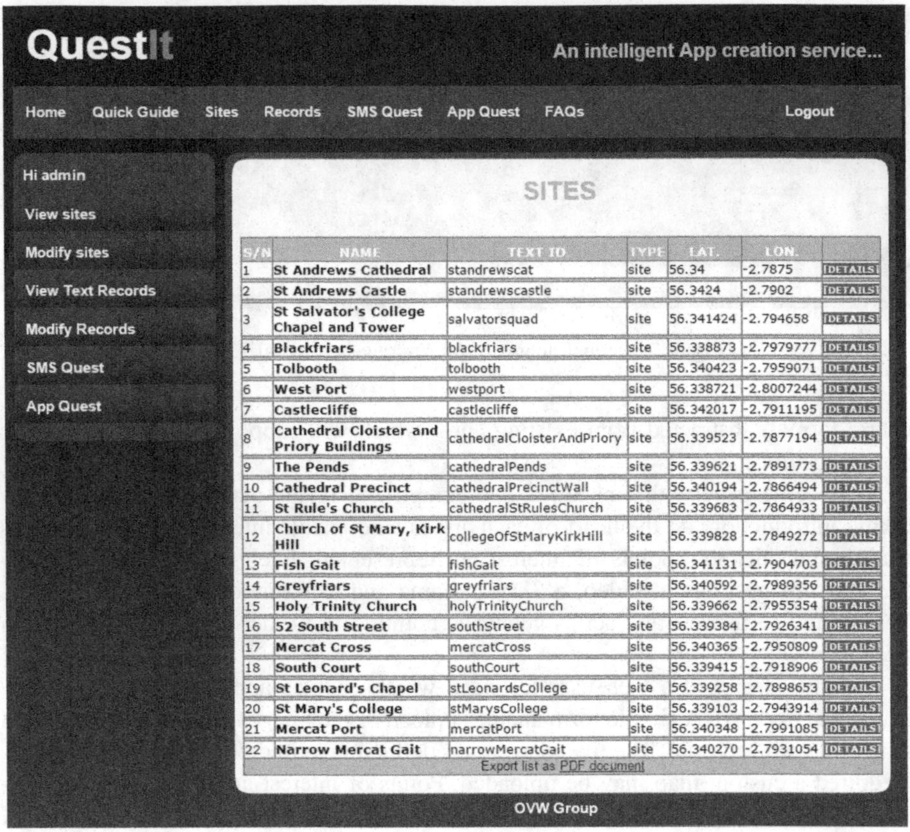

Fig. 5. Administrators interface

information and monitor end user transactions. End Users: These are tourists, passers-by and members of the general public that are interested in learning about the cultural heritage of a given locality. They interact with the system by sending and receiving SMS messages on their mobile devices, and by using the mobile application developed.

The system is made up of the following five components. The knowledgebase: A structured repository that holds all the information used by the system. The SMS inference engine: A set of rules for making deductions based on the contents of the knowledgebase. The GSM modem: A modem that facilitates the receipt and sending of SMS messages from and to users respectively. The administrator's interface: A web interface that provides administrative functionalities such as creating trails, modifying trails and viewing records of SMS transactions. The mobile application: An application that users can download onto their mobile devices (smartphones, tablets, PDAs) to take their learning experience further.

The architecture of the system is shown in Figs. 2 and 3. System administrators and end users access the administrators interface and the mobile application respectively

Fig. 6. Screen shots from the App

over the Internet. However, the SMS functionality of the system is accessed over the cellular (GSM) infrastructure and works independent of Internet access. The GSM modem is connected to an inference engine (which can be configured, started and stopped by the system administrator) connected to the knowledgebase.

An inference engine was developed in Java to facilitate connectivity between the GSM modem that sends and receives SMS messages from users and the server that the modem is connected to. The GSM modem used is the Wavecom Q2303A Module USB GSM Modem. An open-source Java API (SMSLib) was employed in the development of the inference engine to facilitate the AT command-driven communication between the server and GSM modem. This API was then leveraged by writing Java methods and classes to enable the server establish communication with the connected modem, instruct the modem to read incoming messages in real-time as they are being sent by users, generate appropriate responses based on the contents of the received messages, and automatically send those responses to users.

The following steps take place when a user sends an SMS message to the mobile number controlled by the GSM modem:

- User sends SMS message containing text string.
- Modem receives SMS message asynchronously and generates a notification to the inference engine.
- Inference engine connects to the knowledgebase and searches for the text string in stringid column of the trailpoints table. If a match is found, inference engine retrieves the content of the description column of the trailpoints table and stores it in a temporary variable. If no match is found, inference engine generates an "unrecognised string" message and stores it in temporary variable.
- The inference engine instructs the modem to send the contents of the temporary variable as an SMS to the user.
- Modem sends the appropriate response to the user.
- The inference engine stores the transaction details in the records table and updates the users table of the knowledgebase.

2.2   Administrators Web Interface

To ensure accessibility and ease of use, the administrators interface was designed using web technologies and hosted on a server accessible over the Internet. This interface took the form of a dynamic website designed using PHP (for the server-side scripting) and HTML, Javascript and CSS for the client-side. The interface contains functionalities to create trails by adding (as well as deleting and modifying) a series of connected sites and keeping track of end user usage by viewing records of SMS transactions. When adding a site, an administrator specifies the name (e.g. St Andrews Cathedral), a unique string identifier (e.g. "standrewscat"), a description of the site (history, important features, current state and so on), the latitude and longitude coordinates (e.g. 56.34, -2.7875), any additional text (e.g. riddles, quotes or facts associated with the site) and may choose to upload additional resources like images (modern, historic and virtual images of the site), audio files (songs or stories associated with the site) and video files (ancient footage or virtual worlds reconstruction of the site). Once the submit button is clicked, the information specified is validated and then stored in the respective tables in the knowledgebase, and will appear as a site in the administrators web interface. The interface also features a brief introduction and guide on how to use the system and a page devoted to Frequently Asked Questions (FAQs).

Fig. 7. App front

Fig. 8. Using mirrorshades X reality system

2.3   Mobile App

A mobile application has been developed to take users' experience further by leveraging the features and capabilities of smartphones to deliver interactive and engaging contents to users (Fig. 6). To ensure accessibility across multiple mobile platforms (Android, IOS, Windows Mobile, Blackberry, Symbian and so on), PhoneGap was leveraged to build a mobile application using Javascript, HTML5 and CSS3 and then compile the codes for these platforms.

The mobile application connects to the MySQL knowledgebase and reads the contents of the trailpoints and resources tables. This communication is facilitated in Javascript by generating JSON (JavaScript Object Notation) and AJAX (Asynchronous JavaScript and XML) requests to PHP scripts (hosted on an online server) which make SQL queries to the knowledgebase, retrieve data and send the data (encoded as JSON objects) to the client device. The contents of these tables (which represent connected site entities and informative resources associated with these entities) are then visually represented in the mobile application in form of a "heritage map view" and a "sites view". The map view features a series of clickable icons that represent three categories of entities – heritage sites (e.g. St Andrews Cathedral), heritage organisations (e.g. Museum of the University of St Andrews) and the user's location (represented by the coordinates of the user's mobile device) – all on a live map sourced from googlemaps API, with the option of cached offline map tiles (created using Mobile Atlas Creator) available to fall back on in the absence of Internet access. The map view allows users to view the locations of sites and heritage organisations respective to their locations, and interact with a heritage map of the given locality by panning, zooming and clicking on icons to gather more information. The location of each site icon on the map corresponds to the latitude/longitude coordinates specified by the system administrators when creating the site using the web interface, and when a site icon is clicked, users are directed to a page which displays the information associated with the site. The information displayed for each site correspond to the contents specified by the system administrator when creating the site (using the web interface) and includes a text description, image galleries, audio and video playlists, 3D panorama/model, chunks of

Fig. 9. St Salvators geddy view

Fig. 10. St Salvators reconstruction

Fig. 11. St Salvators today

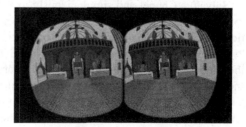

Fig. 12. St Salvators stereoscopic altar

text, latitude/longitude coordinates as well as a button that displays the location of the site on the map view when clicked. Both the map view and sites view have buttons that users click to change their view (e.g. navigate from the map view to the sites), as well as buttons to navigate to the welcome screen point and log out of the system. The following steps outline the flow of information between the administrators interface, mobile application and system resources:

- System administrator creates sites, specifying the name, description, coordinates and multimedia resources using web interface.
- Sites are stored in the knowledgebase.
- User with a smartphone or tablet launches the mobile application and mobile application makes JSON request to PHP script on a web server.
- PHP script queries trailpoints and resources tables of knowledgebase using SQL statements, encodes the retrieved information as JSON objects and transmits the objects.
- Mobile device receives JSON objects, formats them using JavaScript and visualises them on an interactive map view and sites view.

3   Into the Third Dimension with Mirror Shades

We have created 3D reconstructions of a number of medieval buildings in St Andrews. These reconstructions have been used in schools and public exhibitions to provide a new perspective on the past. Users are able to explore these reconstructions through the proxy of an avatar controlled by a key board and mouse or games controller. The models contain interactive content and non-player characters representing personalities from the past such as Robert the Bruce and Cardinal Beaton. These models have also been used to enrich mobile exploration of St Andrews. Images and videos of the reconstruction provide content for the text trails which may be accessed through Web references. The app also has 3D content linked into it. Images of the reconstruction enable comparison with the present day sites as well as with images from the past such as the Geddy map. Videos such as (https://vimeo.com/77928887) enable guided tours of the reconstructions to be followed whilst on site. These provide a valuable but cut down experience of 3D reconstruction but have the benefit of being available on site.

The Mirrorshades cross reality system is based upon the Oculus Rift, Web Cams and an indoor positioning system. This enables users to walk around the current day site of St Salvators Chapel and simultaneously to see the reconstruction of the chapel in stereoscopic 3D. This gives an immersive experience far superior to viewing via a traditional monitor. A challenge for this sort of cross reality system is how to overcome the "vacancy problem" where the user is cognitively present in one reality but absent from the other. We overcome this problem in part by automating navigation. As the user moves around the real space their viewpoint in the virtual space is changed automatically. The user is also able to easily switch between realities at any time. The video cameras provide a view into the real whilst the simulation provides a view into the past. In this way the user is freed to explore the past and to compare it to the current site.

This video shows the mirror shades system in use during an evaluation session where it is used for mobile exploration of St Salvators Chapel.

Mirrorshades has been used to enable comparison of St Salvators chapel as it is today and as it was in the 15th Century. System performance measurements showed that framerates of between 40 and 40 fps were achieved, that latency from cameras was around 180 ms and that user position was tracked to within a few meters whilst moving and to within a meter whilst stationary.

An X-Box controller enabled users to switch between realities, by pushing a button or puling a trigger. There was a preference for alternating between real and virtual rather than viewing both simultaneously. The virtual was viewed more while stationary and the real was moving. The combination of easy switching and intuitive navigation effectively addressed the vacancy problem enabling easy comparison between the two realities. The strength of the immersive experience provided by stereoscopic vision, compensated for the low specs, in terms of framerate, resolution and accuracy of movement tracking provided by the system. All users found the experience to be extremely positive, enjoyable and informative.

4 Conclusion

This paper has outlined three approaches to mobile exploration of Medieval St Andrews. In each case users are able to explore the past and to compare recon-structions and historic images with present days site. The text approach has the advantage of simplicity, intimacy and low tech requirements. Digital literacies exist across the population with respect to texting. Also texts are often seen as high value communication items. The system enables the creation of Quests, where the user progresses from site to site.

The predominance of smart phones equipped with multimedia capabilities, broadband and geo-location systems under pines the creation of the Mediaeval St Andrews app. A visitor or student is able to locate points of interest that are close to them, receive directions on how to reach the point of interest and access a wealth of material about the site. This will include audio commentary, images and text. A valu-able aspect of the app architecture is the inclusion of a web interface which enables the content to be created by filling in forms and uploading files. Consequently given appropriate content it is possible to create a trail app in a short period of time without specialist skills. The third mode of exploration Mirrorshades, enables a fully immersive experience to be achieved on site. The system addresses the vacancy problem and facilitates rich comparison of the present day with the past.

References

Ajinomoh, O., Miller, A., Dow, L., Gordon-Gibson, A., Burt, E., Helfert, M., Martins, M.J., Cordeiro, J. (eds.): Managing humanitarian emergencies - teaching and learning with a virtual humanitarian disaster tool. In: CSEDU, vol. 1, pp. 55–56. SciTePress (2012)

Davies, C., Alan, M., Colin, A.: Mobile cross reality for on-site exploration of cultural heritage reconstructions. In Proceedings of the First International Congress on Digital Cultural Heritage (2013)

Dawson, T., Vermehren, A., Miller, A., Kennedy, S., Oliver, I.: Digitally enhanced community rescue archaeology. In: Proceedings of first International Congress on Digital Heritage (2013)

Dow, L., Campbell, A., Miller, A., McCaffery, J., Oliver, I.A., Kennedy, S., Allison, C.: An immersive platform for collaborative projects. In: Proceedings of IEEE Conference on Frontiers in Education (2014)

Fawcett, R.: The architecture of the Scottish medieval Church. Yale University Press, New York (2011)

Fawcett, R., Foster, S., Tabraham, C.J.: St Andrews Cathedral. Historic, Scotland (2003)

Fawcett, R., Rutherford, A.: Renewed life for Scottish Castles. Council for British Archaeology, New York (2011)

Getchell, K., Miller, A., Allison, C., Sweetman, R.: Serious Games on the Move, chapter Exploring the Second Life of a Byzantine Basilica, pp. 165–180. Springer, Wien (2009)

Getchell, K., Miller, A., Nicoll, J.R., Sweetman, R., Allison, C.: Games methodologies and immersive environments for virtual fieldwork. IEEE Trans. Learn. Technol. **3**, 281–293 (2010)

McCaffery, J., Miller, A., Vermehren, A., Leffery, C., Strikland, K.: Exploring heritage through time and space: supporting community reflection on the highland clearances. In: Proceedings of the First International Congress on Digital Cultural Heritage (2013)

McCaffery, J., Miller, A., Oliver, I.A.: Measurement of immersive technology for historic scenes. In: Proceedings of the 14th Eurographics workshop on Cultural Heritage (2014)

McCaffery, J., Miller, A., Oliver, I., Allison, C.: Augmented learning roads for internet routing. In: Proceedings of IEEE Frontiers in Education (2014)

Miller, A., Dow, L., Kennedy, S., Fawcett, R.: Exploring cultural heritage with open virtual worlds: the reconstruction of St andrews cathedral in opensimulator. In Proceedings of the International Congress on Digital Herritage (2013)

Oliver, I.A., Miller, A.H.D., Allison, C.: Virtual worlds, real traffic: interaction and adaptation. In: Proceedings of the First Annual ACM SIGMM Conference on Multimedia Systems (2010)

Oliver, I., Miller, A., Allison, C.: Mongoose: throughput redistributing virtual world In: Proceedings of the 21st IEEE International Conference on Computer Communication Networks (ICCCN 2012) IEEE (2012)

Oliver, I., Miller, A., Allison, C., Kennedy, S., Dow, L., Campbell, A., Davies, C., McCaffery, J.: Towards the 3D Web with Open Simulator. In: IEEE 27th International Conference on Advanced Information Networking and Applications (2013)

Theoretical Issues for Game-based Virtual Heritage

Erik Champion[(⊠)]

School of Media Culture and Creative Arts, Faculty of Humanities,
Curtin University, Perth, Australia
erik.champion@curtin.edu.au

Abstract. This paper critiques essential features in prominent theories of serious games, and compares them to interaction features of commercial computer games that could be used for history and heritage-based learning in order to develop heuristics that may help future the specific requirements of serious game design for interactive history and digital heritage.

Keywords: Heritage · History · Serious games

1 Definitions of Games

Thomas Malone's paper, *Heuristics for designing enjoyable user interfaces: Lessons from computer games* [1], was an attempt to understand why games are "captivating" and how they can be "used to make other user interfaces interesting and enjoyable to use." In order to answer this question he set up three empirical studies (but only describes two), and takes away "motivational features" to see which features add the most to captivation. Malone asked eight groups of ten students to play a computer game (called "Darts"), and then another game ("Hangman") but with one of eight features missing. He recorded how long played each game (completion time), their personal opinions (as to which game they preferred), and their gender.

In his second study, using a similar method, Malone found that explicit goals, scorekeeping, audio effects, and randomness were particularly important. These two studies were then followed in his paper by the claim that challenge, fantasy, and curiosity were the important ingredients that make games captivating and fun to use. More recent publications, such as a doctoral thesis by Federoff [2], and other papers [3–5] have stressed the importance of Malone's paper in explaining the unique features of games, how they differ in the way they are experienced from other types of software, and from typical HCI, and how a new set of heuristics is needed to address these specific game features.

In contrast to typical software design aims, Malone's paper reminds us that our quest is to create more challenging environments, (and challenge in the sense of a difficulty people wish to face, not wish to avoid). There is an often-overlooked gap between games and other software, for games are not just efficient rules-based systems. Malone explained that HCI traditionally seeks to improve software that is easy to learn and easy to master, but notes the founder of Atari said games are designed to be easy to

© Springer International Publishing Switzerland 2015
M. Ebner et al. (Eds): EiED 2014, CCIS 486, pp. 125–136, 2015.
DOI: 10.1007/978-3-319-22017-8_11

learn but difficult to master. Malone argued that computer games are more like toys than other software applications, which in turn are more like tools.

Games have goals but they do not have to have clear outcomes. They do however incorporate challenge and fantasy, and stimulate curiosity. Malone's paper defined challenge as involving "a goal whose outcome is uncertain," as there is often variable difficulty level or multiple goals (potentially distributed over different levels). Fantasy incorporates emotionally appealing features, or well-mapped cognitive metaphors. Curiosity is seen as "optimal level of information complexity." It may incorporate randomness or contextual humour.

Malone was perceptive enough to realize that challenge is not merely about making things difficult, but also making these barriers tantalizing to solve. For example, when the author evaluated [6] over eighty people and how they learn about the original inhabitants through exploring virtual reconstructions of archaeological sites, he asked the users if the environments were challenging without realizing this subtle distinction. The users were confused as to whether he meant challenging as in "this is difficult, I am not sure I can or want to complete it", or "this is really testing me but I really don't want to do anything else until I crack it." This second meaning of challenging is an important feature of a successful game; it affords hard fun.

Gestalt theory seems to be behind Malone's concept of curiosity as a motivating feature of games, he suggested users want to have 'well formed knowledge structures," that games deliberately suggest such knowledge but present the "knowledge structure" as incomplete, inconspicuous or unparsimonious (by this he may have meant games provide red herrings or an overflow of potential clues).

Like Malone, James Gee [7] reiterates that games are "hard fun" but also that games are successful because game designers also have to learn the hard way, success in game design is through trial and error, ensuring that the very design of the game helps people learn them in a challenging but enjoyable way. Their income depends on it. This may seem obvious, but Gee also says something fascinating, that games are good "if you act like a game designer while you play the game." While thinking and talking about games is important, one should not have to think like a designer to enjoy a game. If you design objects, events and spaces so that people have to think like you to have "good experiences" then the richness and variety of potential experiences have been lost.

Another potential confusion in reading Gee's work is that he emphasizes the advantages possible with games as if they are inherent in all games. For example, Gee wrote that "good games are problem solving spaces that create deep learning" and that "good video games are hard work, deep fun and provide "good learning" for other contexts, i.e. transferrable knowledge. "Tetris", "Pac-Man", and "Space Invaders", are often considered to be good games, but they don't appear to fulfil all three of the above criteria. And yet it would seem, following Gee, that good games have to always create "deep learning" and if games are sometimes tools then they must always be "…new tools for letting people understand from the inside out the worlds other people inhabit or worlds no one has seen yet." Unfortunately Gee seems to be conflating the apparent potential of computer games with the current state of computer games.

Anderson et al. [8] and Dondlinger [9] defined a game as essentially an activity that: has some goal in mind, the player works to achieve; has systematic or emergent rules; and is considered a form of play or competition. While this encompasses "skill and drill" types of games, many of today's digital games are much more complex, providing an interactive narrative in which the player must test hypotheses, synthesize knowledge, and respond to the unexpected [9]. Games also don't have to provide the rules, part of the challenge might be to find them, and predict what will happen next according to the player's understanding of what the rules are.

Juul [10] defined a game as "a rule-based formal system with a variable and quantifiable outcome, where different outcomes are assigned different values, the player exerts effort in order to influence the outcome, the player feels attached to the outcome, and the consequences of the activity are optional and negotiable." While plausible on first reading, the rules of the game are the rules of the designer or even the rules of the player. The negotiation, changes, and misunderstandings as to what are the rules exactly are, by the player, is an important and creative part of games, and by extension, computer games. If you believe the essence of the game is a rules-based system, you might not consider the possibility that even for a game a rule system could be random, changing, or open to change by the player.

Salen and Zimmerman [11] wrote "A game is a system in which players engage in an artificial conflict, defined by rules, that results in a quantifiable outcome." Such definitions of computer games as systems do not address why users find games enjoyable and do not directly lead us to producing better games that users enjoy more. Salen and Zimmerman's definition also discounts games that may never have a final outcome (such as cricket), and does not incorporate the importance of strategy. As we have seen, rules do not fully encapsulate games, they may be necessary components, but there may be games entered where the rules on entry are redefined while playing. So here is an alternative definition of a computer game:

A computer game is an engaging challenge that offers up the possibility of temporary or permanent tactical resolution without harmful outcomes to the real world situation of the participant.

This working definition may not appear to be exacting enough; it seems to treat all games as challenge, when the challenge element is not necessarily of the same importance in all games; and it emphasizes tactics when not all games require changing tactics and strategies. But if the game does not offer strategic resolution, then it is no longer offering a full and rich game; it is almost a game-shell, or a game-vehicle. The procedures are the same but the game is no longer enjoyable and engaging.

Papert [12] stated that games are not fun because they are easy; they are fun because they are difficult to learn. Creating something that is easy is not making something engaging. Secondly, Papert thinks that educational games that hide their true intention are misleading if not immoral. Further, games allow and in fact demand agency and effort from the player, and provide clear feedback and reward systems. Therefore Paper encourages two things, conversation between the players, and encouraging them to "become game designers themselves."

Ian Bogost is probably most famously associated with the phrase *procedural rhetoric*. Bogost [13] defined procedural rhetoric as "a practice of using processes persuasively." Bogost himself raises a potential flaw; he admits that for many people rhetoric has a negative connotation. For example, in *Arguing well*, John Shand [14] declared "Logic must be sharply distinguished from what might generally be called rhetoric… rhetoric is not committed to using good arguments".

Miguel Sicart [15] wrote: "Proceduralists claim that players, by reconstructing the meaning embedded in the rules, are persuaded by virtue of the games' procedural nature." Sicart argued that meaning is more than just the learning of rules through play, the value of gameplay is made subservient, and if rules are all that matter why should the designers have to explain them? There is another concern here (depending on whether are we supposed to question the system of or not). Adherence to the altar of "procedural rhetoric", whether intended by Bogost, or not, can lead to people thinking that the designer's idea of the game rules are what matters.

There has also been some criticism of Bogost's other (but related) book, *Unit Operations* [16]. Alex Wade [17] wrote "description of ancient videogames Pong and Combat as games with 'tennislike attributes' (59) stretches the membrane of the operation of units beyond perspicuity and into the realm of fiction." How can procedural rhetoric be employed in designing serious games? While Bogost seems to be saying we have to understand procedural rhetoric, astute critics and game designers do not seem sure as to how they can implement these theoretical notions [18].

2 Narrative and Historical Reality

So how can we use games for history? At a very basic level we can distinguish them as follows. Games can be used discursively to play and answer questions. The classroom can play them in a group or individually and then present their viewpoints on authenticity or character motivation to the class. Secondly, games are performative, but they can also be performative in a more general sense. Students could role-play game characters, with puppets, or as actors or as narrators, and could film their historical interpretations as machinima (film created by the in-game cameras). Thirdly, at least some games are thesis-based kitset visualization and simulation machines; they can help structure and procedurally test theories as to how cities and empires are formed. Players can mod cities and empires events based on interpretative theories inside games that are moddable, or sandbox games.

Many are using and testing the portrayal of history in games through their history class or in their research [19], while at the other end of the spectrum the same games have endured some considerable criticism by practicing historians. For example, the famous historian Niall Ferguson [20] wrote in the New York Mag, "Civilization and Empire Earth, to take perhaps the best-known examples, are not what the historian needs, since what they provide is such a crude caricature of the historical process."

Despite these criticisms, games are growing in popularity, and many cultural heritage projects have harnessed game technology and techniques. The heritage projects may use a game engine [21] or be games in the fuller sense of the word [22] and there have been recent surveys on games appropriate to cultural heritage [23]. To counter the burgeoning interest in games, there have also been papers warning of game ideas applied to cultural heritage with disastrous results [24].

Using powerful game engines may help us prototype digital representations of virtual heritage environments in a medium accessible to a generation less appreciative of books, but these games carry "genre baggage". Even first year archaeology students are keen to find out what they can destroy in these virtual environments designed to show them past artefacts in use [6, 25]. They are accustomed to games, and may attempt to do the same destructive things in game-based historical environments. This problem of using a toy as a tool is something the author has previously described as the "Indiana Jones dilemma" [26], where the popular media presentation of archaeology dramatically increases its popularity while diminishing the public understanding of what archaeologists actually do.

This dilemma worsens the more we have actual user-accessible interactive content to model, something not shared with traditional, flythrough, and instructor-controlled, virtual environments. The more interactive the content, the more visitors will want to manipulate or even sabotage it. In the author's own 2004 evaluations of archaeology students and visualization experts, he found that game genres are both a blessing and a curse [6]. When told a virtual environment is a game, participants of all ages and both genders seem much more at ease and aware of potential affordances. However, they tend to look for interaction and personalization while disregarding the actual content, and they conflate fact, conjecture and fiction, when a discursive and contestable simulation may actually be the preferred option [27].

It could be counter-argued that computer games featuring history and heritage can be used and interacted with in a meaningful way by teachers and students (which is the argument of McCall [19]). It also depends on the interrelation of teacher and student, and blended learning may not fully immerse the student in the "there" of virtual heritage environments. For example, Gaver et al. [28] wrote that the games differed from typical software: "If a system can easily be used to achieve practical tasks, this will distract from the possibilities it offers for more playful engagement."

Game designers may also be led to believe that games using historical characters, events, or settings are readily adaptable and immediately appropriate to virtual heritage, and many have made the case for using game engines for virtual heritage projects [29–31] but there are fundamental conceptual issues still to be addressed. To what extent is the past more or less important or retrievable than history, and how is it attainable through interaction (as otherwise there is little point to using virtual environments)? One answer may be adopting virtual reality to represent the past or online digital worlds to represent the future, but it is still too easy to be taken in by the lure of technology and forget to concentrate on enhancing the user experience.

3 Evaluation and Understanding

Evaluating serious games featuring the latest technology raises several issues. When evaluated the user experience of interactive virtual environments, the author was faced with choosing people to compare two virtual environments against each other (subjective preference), or compare the task performance of two different user groups in two different environments. With the first method people typically lack experience in judging virtual environments against each other, for it is such a new technology; with the second method there is no guarantee that the testers' relevant demographic factors would be spread relatively evenly across the two groups.

A very simple rule of thumb to uncover whether a game or virtual environment helps a meaningful learning experience is to ask (based on the data available), what do you want or expect the audience to learn? Which interaction method best achieves this? Does the resulting simulation add a new perspective, which would be more difficult to design and deliver in other media? How can this new knowledge be used, communicated, and transferred beyond the game? Does the knowledge also help uncover the process by which the original data was first interpreted, or does it help the audience (students and teachers, general public and scholars) to critique the ways this knowledge is typically presented and experienced?

Would a socially situated role help the audience understand how the place is inhabited and experienced? For example, a warrior might learn about weapon features, landscape advantages and disadvantages, a command system, wayfinding, or the privileges of ranks. A thief might also learn about hiding places, but also about where people go and when, they are on guard, where valuables are stored. A druid might learn about the cultivation of herbs, astronomy, medicine, and so on. A merchant might need to learn about artefacts, the value of objects, certain ways of counting, the location of valuable items, barter methods, trade distances, dangers, foreign language and appropriate behaviour, optimal travel routes, and so on. The challenge is to match the knowledge to be provided with the interaction suitable to both the game and the audience.

Another interesting issue in game-based learning is in research into whether computer games can add to or will only distract student attention span. There is a school of thought in archaeology that disregards the learning capabilities of digital media, seeing visualization as purely a shop façade or even distraction for the serious and scholarly pastime of reading and writing books [32]. Yet if we avoid teaching with digital media, how will the changing attention spans and learning patterns of new generations be best addressed [33]?

So there are many important, perhaps even critical problems in using computer game technology and conventions for virtual heritage environments. Some academics worry about the violence in many computer games, or the time they take away from other pursuits [34]. Others do not believe they test the appropriate cognitive skills. Educators are also concerned that game-style interaction is typically destructive, and not conducive to developing either cultural awareness, or an appreciation of preservation of objects and the cultural values of others.

Evaluating cultural learning is also very difficult [25] so we have looked at using biosensors and brain scanning in tandem with traditional survey questionnaires to gain feedback on what does and does not work. Another option is to adapt digital exercise machines and build tracking devices into tangible interfaces that track individual user preferences and allow the experiences to be shared between individual users and a wider audience [35].

Even if we decide on what we are evaluating, it is not clear how to evaluate. The ethnographic techniques used by researchers may be effective in recording activity, but they do not directly indicate the potential mental transformations of perspective that result from being subjectively immersed in a different type of cultural presence [36]. Real-world tests will not necessarily be of help in assessing heritage reconstructions, unless the virtual experience is supposed to tally as accurately as possible with a given and accessible real-world experience of that culture. This is a problem if the real culture being simulated no longer exists in one place or at the current time, or if the cultural knowledge is fragmented or only circulated among experts and not the general public.

This leads us to the thorny issue of how to evaluate such a concept. We could use questionnaires; we could test the ability of participants to extrapolate general cultural rules or other information and apply them to other heritage sites; we could test whether participants could detect other players or nonplaying characters that appeared to belong to or not belong to the resident culture. We could also test for engagement using questionnaires, by recording physiological data, or by testing the memory recall of the participants. A further option is to give users tasks to complete, and record their performance. However such testing only records their technical proficiency, and not necessarily their cultural understanding.

Applicable research requires continual evaluation via shared tools amongst a body of scholars who agree on suitable goals and methods. To achieve this on-going research activity, the content to be examined must be clearly understood and capable of further analysis. Interaction in a virtual heritage environment requires suitable and appropriate context that communicates the meaning not just of objects but also between objects and their creators.

It is easier to quantify technical advances, and to secure funding to do so, but the mission of virtual heritage is to communicate cultural knowledge, not merely to show it. This may be why we currently have little evidence as to whether virtual heritage environments can afford useful and unique ways for augmenting and evoking aware-ness and understanding of distant places and foreign cultures.

Cultural meaning comes from engagement through cultural presence and education through cultural awareness, understanding and immersion. Critical research needs to be undertaken on the specific abilities of digital media to aid engagement, understanding, and awareness of other cultures. Education, funology, and digital media are not extensively evaluated in combination, but they should be. Evaluation requires defini-tions, guidelines (heuristics), and dependent variables that can be tested (which is difficult in regards to cultural learning), and effectively communicated to designers so that they in turn can effectively transmit cultural information digitally to a varied audience. Hence they need to understand what exactly cultural information is, and how to best communicate it digitally [37].

To increase interest and a sense of inhabitation or specific contextually situated behaviours, a designer could deliberately evoke a sense of cultural presence (as a perceived encounter with digitally simulated cultural agency). However, we do not have agreed definitions of cultural presence and so designers do not have clear ideas, as to which factors which most aid cultural presence, cultural learning, and both proce-dural and discursive archaeological knowledge.

In order to improve the transfer of cultural significance, domain subject experts, such as archaeologists and anthropologists, ought to reconsider not only the technical but also conceptual features of commercial and open-source computer games. Impor-tant features of games include the ability to learn through testing and exploring, the capacity to personalize, annotate, and add content, and the ability of games to challenge people to complete tasks, and try out new strategies, techniques, and identities [38, 39].

Heritage projects are typically designed by experts directly for the general public, but subject matter expertise may blind the designers to the immediate needs of the very audience they are designing for. Subject matter experts may already know the facts, hypotheses, and conjecture as to what was there, what was seen, what was believed, what was done, and what was valued. However, the general public needs to not just learn this, but also develop the desire to learn this knowledge. They will not have the same incentive to read the background information necessary to judge the authenticity and appropriateness of virtual heritage projects.

4 Critical Gaming Checklist

How can we ensure that our critical positions, theories, and arguments about gaming have merit? This is a work-in progress checklist that may help identify weak points in an argument. Ideally a critical position /argument about computer games should be:

1. Falsifiable and verifiable. Not such a common feature in the Humanities, and not always relevant, but in my opinion a good argument should be saying where and when it is contestable, and where and when it can be proven or disproven.
2. Extensible and scalable. We should be able to add to it, extend it, apply it to more research questions and research areas or add it to current research findings or critical frameworks.
3. Reconfigurable. Components are more useful than take it or leave it positions.
4. Is useful even if proven wrong in terms of data, findings, methods, or argument (possibly this heuristic should be combined with number 3).
5. Helpful to the current and future design of computer games, and has potential to forecast future changes in design, deployment or acceptance.
6. Not in danger of conflating describing computer games with prescribing how computer games should be. Several of the arguments cited in this book appear to make that mistake.
7. Understands the distinction between methods and methodology, the selection or rejection of methods should always be examined and communicated.
8. Is lucid and honest about the background, context, and motivations as factors driving it. The parameters of the argument should also be disclosed.
9. Aiming for validity and soundness of argument.
10. Attempting to provide in a long-term and accessible way for the data, output, and results of any experiment or survey to be examinable by others.

This suggestion is corroborated by the method employed in a recent journal article and survey on serious games [40], it determined "high quality" publication by:

- The appropriateness of the research design for addressing the research question.
- The appropriateness of the methods and analysis.
- How generalizable the findings were (with respect to sample size and representativeness).
- The relevance of the focus of the study.
- The extent to which the study findings can be trusted in answering the question(s).

5   Design Implications

Through the game itself, we can also create our own levels that bend space and time. Could we also bend or invert conventional notions of historical narrative? Is it possible to meaningfully do so, and personalize a virtual environment through the interactions that take place within it, even if that interaction initially appears to be destructive? Can we share these meanings within a community, or reveal meanings about a community that is typically removed from us? Given improvements in technology, will these environments improve or hinder a sense of authenticity?

Possible learning mechanics include learning by resource management; learning about social behaviour (chat, observation, mimicry); visualization of scale, landscape or climate; depicting varying levels of uncertainty; allowing visitors to filter or reconfigure reconstructions; immersion in the excitement of the times; selecting correct objects or appearance to move about the 'world' or to trade or to advance social role or period of time; deciphering codes, language, avoiding traps; and online walkthroughs.

The major theories in game design that concentrate on serious games may all need to be re-examined and re-adjusted for interactive history and virtual heritage. For historical simulations we may wish for players to understand the rules, and debate them, or learn how to extrapolate from them. For heritage, while we may wish for players to understand or to debate system rules, we are probably going to stress the learning of local culturally constrained perspectives. In such a scenario, the fiction world-real world becomes a local belief-outside belief system. Procedural rhetoric may also lose some of its appeal because the games/interactive environments are likely to be approached as a group, in a museum or similar institution, and so there would be fewer opportunities for continual repetition.

Given the above, historical simulations should endeavour to achieve the following:

- Provide (at some stage of the experience), a framework in which the player (or perhaps, here, participant is a better word) gains an overview of what has been documented, simulated, or construed.
- Convey a sense of the historical context, and the way in which that shaped the actions of the inhabitants.
- Affordances to help participants understand and explain the information in a way that suits them rather than the designer and to allow for different pathways, actions and goal selection.
- Encourage the participants to seek out more information for themselves beyond the historical simulation.

How can we find out how the original inhabitants and historical figures and associated minor characters interacted? Each assortment of historical data and quasi-historical data will differ; there won't be an easy universal solution. However, any historical simulation should have some robust and consistent way to understand the level of engagement and knowledge and curiosity acquired by the simulation. So a further step would be to incorporate a way in which the participants' engagement and acquired conceptual understanding (and/or acquired historical skills) can be ascertained without interrupting the participants' experience and without relying on subjective intervention biased due to subconscious aims of the researcher or designer.

6 Summary

While games and game design principles have and will continue to enrich and inform games designed to educate and disseminate virtual heritage and interactive history, the specific challenges of this research field suggests that new theories as to how people can and should learn are best developed looking at more specifically relevant domains than by extrapolating overarching principles from games in general. Games are not designed according to the aims of generic software, and history and heritage-based games also have specific issues to resolve. As a response, this paper suggested a general definition of a computer game, a working checklist for reviewing theories of game design, and recommendations for developing historical and heritage-based content with computer game themes and elements.

References

1. Malone, T.W.: Heuristics for designing enjoyable user interfaces: lessons from computer games. In: Proceedings of the 1982 Conference on Human Factors in Computing Systems, pp. 63–68. ACM (1982)
2. Federoff, M.A.: Heuristics and usability guidelines for the creation and evaluation of fun in video games. Citeseer (2002)
3. Jørgensen, A.H.: Marrying HCI/usability and computer games: a preliminary look. In: Proceedings of the Third Nordic Conference on Human-Computer Interaction, pp. 393–396. ACM (2004)
4. Desurvire, H., Caplan, M., Toth, J.A.: Using heuristics to evaluate the playability of games. In: CHI 2004 Extended Abstracts on Human factors in computing systems, pp. 1509–1512. ACM (2004)
5. Shneiderman, B.: Designing for fun: how can we design user interfaces to be more fun? Interactions **11**, 48–50 (2004)
6. Champion, E.: Playing With The Past. Springer, Heidelberg (2011)
7. Gee, J.P.: Good Video Games Plus Good Learning. Peter Lang, New York (2007)
8. Anderson, E.F., McLoughlin, L., Liarokapis, F., Peters, C., Petridis, P., Freitas, S.: Developing serious games for cultural heritage: a state-of-the-art review. Virtual Real. **14**, 255–275 (2010)
9. Dondlinger, M.J.: Educational video games design. a review of the literature. J. Appl Educ. Technol. **4**, 21–31 (2007)
10. Juul, J.: Half-real: Video Games Between Real Rules and Fictional Worlds. The MIT Press, Cambridge, MA (2011)
11. Salen, K., ZImmerman, E.: Rules of Play Game Design Fundamentals. The MIT Press, Cambridge (2003)
12. Papert, S.: Does Easy Do It? Children, Games, and Learning. Game Developer, Soapbox section 88 (1998)

13. Bogost, I.: Persuasive Games: The Expressive Power of Videogames. MIT Press, Cambridge, MA (2007)
14. Shand, J.: Arguing Well. Routledge, London (2002)
15. Sicart, M.: Against procedurality. Game Stud. Int. J. Comput. Game Res. 11 (2011)
16. Bogost, I.: Unit Operations: An Approach to Videogame Criticism. MIT Press, Cambridge (2008)
17. Wade, A.: Unit operations: an approach to videogame criticism – Ian Bogost. Sociol. Rev. **55**, 181–184 (2007)
18. Whalen, Z.: Unit operations: an approach to videogame criticism gameology: a scholarly community dedicated to the study of videogames. Review of Bogost, Ian (2006)
19. McCall, J.: Gaming the Past: Using Video Games to Teach Secondary History. Routledge, New York (2013)
20. Ferguson, N.: How to Win a War. New York News and Politics. NYMag.com, Online (2006)
21. Bellotti, F., Berta, R., De Gloria, A., Panizza, G., Primavera, L.: Designing cultural heritage contents for serious virtual worlds. In: VSMM 2009 15th International Conference on Virtual Systems and Multimedia, pp. 227–231 (2009)
22. Chen, S., Pan, Z., Zhang, M., Shen, H.: A case study of user immersion-based systematic design for serious heritage games. Multimed. Tools Appl. **62**, 633–658 (2013)
23. Mikovec, Z., Slavik, P., Zara, J.: Cultural heritage, user interfaces and serious games at CTU prague. In: VSMM 2009 15th International Conference on Virtual Systems and Multimedia, pp. 211–216 (2009)
24. Leader-Elliott, L.: Community heritage interpretation games: a case study from Angaston, South Australia. Inte. J. Herit. stud. **11**, 161–171 (2005)
25. Champion, E., Bishop, I., Dave, B.: The Palenque project: evaluating interaction in an online virtual archaeology site. Virtual Real. **16**, 121–139 (2012)
26. Champion, E.: Indiana Jones and the joystick of doom: understanding the past via computer games. In: Traffic, vol. 5, pp. 47–65 (2004)
27. Kensek, K., Swartz, D.L., Cipolla, N.: Fantastic reconstructions or reconstructions of the fantastic? tracking and presenting ambiguity, alternatives, and documentation in virtual worlds. In: ACADIA 2002 Thresholds between Physical and Virtual Conference, pp. 293–306. ACADIA (2002)
28. Gaver, W.W., Bowers, J., Boucher, A., Gellerson, H., Pennington, S., Schmidt, A., Steed, A., Villars, N., Walker, B.: The drift table: designing for ludic engagement. In: CHI 2004 Extended Abstracts on Human Factors in Computing Systems, pp. 885–900. ACM (2004)
29. Bottino, A., Martina, A.: The role of computer games industry and open source philosophy in the creation of affordable virtual heritage solutions. In: Er, M.J. (ed.) (2010)
30. Lucey-Roper, M.: Discover Babylon: creating a vivid user experience by exploiting features of video games and uniting museum and library collections. In: Proceedings Archives and Museum Informatics Museums and the Web 2006, Toronto (2006)
31. Stone, R.J.: Serious gaming - virtual reality's saviour?. In: Conference on VSMM 2005, pp. 773–786. Ename, Belgium (2005)
32. Parry, R.: Digital heritage and the rise of theory in museum computing. Mus. Manag. Curatorship **20**, 333–348 (2005)
33. Mehegan, D.: Young people reading a lot less: report laments the social costs, vol. 2008. The Boston Globe, Boston (2007)
34. Yee, N.: The labor of fun: how video games blur the boundaries of work and play. Games Cult. **1**, 68–71 (2006)
35. Dourish, P.: Where the Action is: The Foundations of Embodied Interaction. MIT Press, Cambridge (2001)

36. Benford, S., Fraser, M.E.A.: Staging and evaluating public performances as an approach to CVE research. In: Proceedings of the 4th International Conference on Collaborative Virtual Environments. ACM Press (2002)
37. Mulholland, P., Collins, T.: Using digital narratives to support the collaborative learning and exploration of cultural heritage. In: 2002 Proceedings 13th International Workshop on Database and Expert Systems Applications, pp. 527–531. IEEE (2002)
38. Boellstorff, T.: A ludicrous discipline? Ethnography and game studies. Games Cult. 1, 29–35 (2006)
39. Johnson, S.: Everything Bad is Good for You: How Popular Culture is Making us Smarter. Penguin Books, Bristol (2005). Allen Lane
40. Connolly, T.M., Boyle, E.A., MacArthur, E., Hainey, T., Boyle, J.M.: A systematic literature review of empirical evidence on computer games and serious games. Comput. Educ. 59, 661–686 (2012)

Author Index

Printed in the United States
by Bookmasters

Printed in the United States
By Bookmasters